Advance prai~~ ior
The Boxer

Ron Smith has written a brave and honest account of a life well lived, with his number one supporter and wife Sharyn by his side playing an integral part in his success.

His story reveals his many regrets, but also his determination to make up for them. When the Dalai Lama said, "When you lose, don't lose the lesson", Ron listened. He gained much by recognising his mistakes and moving forward – setting goals and following through. In doing so he has lifted himself, and so many others, to greater heights.

As he writes in this remarkable memoir, "I'd much prefer to train a young person to become a champion person rather than a champion boxer." Well done, Champ – you do that in spades.

– Julie Davey | Director at A for Attitude | CEO and board member at Attitude Books Foundation Inc. | Author of *A for Attitude*

This is a captivating journey. Written with, at times, raw honesty and heartfelt intent. From start to finish I was entertained, uplifted and inspired. A courageous tale well told. This is simply a 'must read' for any man looking to learn and grow into another level.

– Troy Jones | Founder and CEO at Real Men Project | Founder of Pregnant Pause | Author of *Being Dad*

An amazing story about an amazing man with an amazing life. Knowing Ron only over more recent years, as a gentle fitness fanatic, I found it almost unbelievable to read about darker times in his past. His story is a lesson in overcoming adversity, and that anything can be achieved with passion and discipline (and Sharyn, of course)! This book is a great keepsake for his large family. I look forward to him writing an updated edition in 30 years' time!

– Dr Joshua Honig

A great read, made more personal because of our weekly personal training sessions. Although not an elite athlete, I was able to relate to the self-sacrifice, dedication and commitment necessary to achieve outside of your comfort zone.

It was very brave of Ron to expose himself 'warts and all' ... 'the good, the bad and the ugly'. He has outlined the roller-coaster journey of his life and that at times it was uncontrollable and frightening. In so doing, however, he has demonstrated that achievement is possible for us all.

The average person can be empowered and fulfilled with success despite adversity and misfortune. Ron is a great role model, and will no doubt continue to positively influence those who come into contact with him.

An essential book for those who lack the confidence, or know-how, to improve their lives.

– Dr Jack Knobel

The Boxer

My Journey to Lifelong Health and Fitness

Ron Smith

This is an IndieMosh book

brought to you by MoshPit Publishing
an imprint of Mosher's Business Support Pty Ltd

PO Box 147
Hazelbrook NSW 2779

indiemosh.com.au

Cataloguing-in-Publication entry is available from the National Library of Australia: http://catalogue.nla.gov.au/

Title:	The Boxer: My Journey to Lifelong Health and Fitness
Author:	Smith, Ron (1944–)
ISBNs:	978-1-925739-97-8 (paperback)
	978-1-925739-85-5 (ebook – epub)
	978-1-925739-86-2 (ebook – mobi)

Cover design and layout by Ally Mosher at allymosher.com

Cover photo courtesy of Yanni.

All other photos are from the author's private collection unless otherwise acknowledged.

The Robert Evans quote appears unmodified courtesy of wikiquotes.com under Creative Commons License Attribution – Share Alike 3.0 Unported (CC BY-SA 3.0) found at https://creativecommons.org/licenses/by-sa/3.0/

The Boxer DVD text reproduced with kind permission of Jack Ahern.

Dedication

I dedicate this journey called my life to Sharyn, my soulmate, best friend, lover, wife and business partner. Without Sharyn this story would have ended a long time ago. Thank you for your love, support and honesty; I respect and love you so much.

To my dad, your courage, integrity and class remain with me to this day. You passed away before I could ever appreciate what you taught me and before I could thank you. I often feel your strength within me.

To my six children, Sheree, Kelly, Debbie, Megan, Adam and Rebekah. I love you all so very much. I hope this story helps you to understand the complex individual that is your Dad.

Acknowledgements

Sharyn Smith, thank you for your unwavering support, guidance, help and patience through this often emotional time of self-doubt regarding my ability to follow my dreams and passion to bring this story together. You are my rock. I love you.

Elaine Strong, thank you for your proofreading and comments. You have been a mother figure to me for many years and it has been a privilege to be able to discuss my book with the matriarch of the Strong family.

Judy Finlay, it has been a privilege to have you proofread and provide advice on my story. Thank you for pointing out all the grammar edits required. Sharyn was delighted. Our fitness and friendship journey is now 10 years old and I am so honoured to call you my friend.

Dr Joshua Honig, my doctor, medical advisor and friend of 13 years, thank you for reading and providing a testimonial for my story. You always reassure me and give me a laugh.

Dr Jack Knobel, a personal training client and friend since 2007, thank you for providing a testimonial and kind words.

Troy Jones, Founder and CEO at Real Men Project, Founder of Pregnant Pause and bestselling author of *Being Dad*, thanks for taking time from your busy schedule to read my story and provide a testimonial.

Julie Davey, Director at A for Attitude, CEO and board member at Attitude Books Foundation Inc., thank you for giving me the opportunity to work with you all those years ago and for reading my book and giving your personal review. Julie is an inspirational author and illustrator and was responsible for our very first business logo.

Sheree, Kelly and Debbie, three wonderful women who have given me another chance to be their Dad, thank you so much and I love you all so much.

Adam and Rebekah, I can't thank you enough for your endless love, support and encouragement with all that I have endeavoured to achieve during your lives. You are two special human beings and I am so proud of you and love you more than life itself.

Adam Finlay, I feel so fortunate and grateful that our paths crossed. The common link was your mum, whom I have had the good fortune to train and call my friend. From our first meeting I felt your empathy and understanding. Handing my story over to you for editing was a special moment for me as this manuscript represents my life and I trusted you implicitly. On receiving and reading your finished product I could not be happier with the result; it felt as though I was telling myself my own story. I will be forever grateful for your professionalism and sense of me! Thank you from the bottom of my heart.

Sincere thanks to Jennifer Mosher from IndieMosh for your support, professionalism and advice. Your book *Self publishing for Australian authors* was an invaluable resource to begin our journey and answered so many questions for us. Without you and your team, this book would never have been completed.

The entire process has been smooth and uncomplicated and we have been so impressed by your understanding, support and advice every step of the way.

Thanks also to Samantha for all the edits and Ally for the cover design. We love your work and appreciate all the assistance you have given us during this often confusing journey, more than you'll ever know.

Ron Smith
Mount Eliza, Victoria, 2018

www.lifelonghealthandfitness.com.au
www.mtelizaboxingcentre.net

Contents

There are three sides to every story:
your side, my side and the truth.
And no one is lying.
Memories shared serve each differently.

Robert Evans

My journey to lifelong health and fitness

When I was in my twenties and thirties, I used to say that if I ever went to jail I would write my memoir. Thankfully, I never went to jail and I'm very grateful to have lived such an amazing life.

There have been lots of highs but also many lows and at times I've been ashamed of the choices I've made.

I hope that I've learned lessons, and helped others to bring out the best in themselves.

My journey has been a wild ride and I'm so proud to be able to take you, the reader, along with me in this book. I hope you enjoy it as much as I have enjoyed bringing it to you.

I have had to reflect on many aspects of my life that I'm not proud of and it has had quite a cathartic effect on me.

Fortunately, for the past 40 years, Sharyn (my wife) and I have kept diaries on and off, as did my father during World War II, and I've been able to access considerable information and memories through these records. I've included many short diary excerpts in this book, to capture first-hand how we felt at special times and places.

The writing process hasn't been easy for me, having left school at age 13 and not being very good with English.

But I feel very proud and blessed that I got to 'go ride a horse' and in a roundabout way found a life. You'll have to read on to understand exactly what I mean.

So, my journey to lifelong health and fitness. Here goes!

Chapter 1:
First memories

My first memories are of Mum and Dad bringing my baby sister Glenda home from hospital to our house in Studley Street, Abbotsford, when I was almost five.

Our tiny house had a meter that needed coins to provide electricity to the home, and it always seemed to be a problem for my parents to find the money. I was born in 1944, and my brother Trevor arrived in 1946. Glenda Joy, our little sister, came next in 1949, so by the time I had started to notice the world around me, our house had three children under the age of five. No wonder money seemed a bit tight.

I can also remember my football going flat at school in Grade 1 at Cromwell State School in 1950. Thinking that it was no good anymore I put it into the school incinerator. When I arrived home without it my mum and her sister, Auntie Josie, took me back to school to retrieve it.

Mum was born in 1919 as Margaret Elizabeth Martin, and had two sisters – the older Audrey and my Auntie Josephine, who was feisty enough to enjoy the opportunity to drag me back to school for my lost possessions.

At the back of our tiny yard was a gate that opened onto a small lane. Most of the houses in the area seemed to have a laneway at the back of the property. Out of the gate and across the lane lived two good friends of Mum and Dad, Eddie and Edith Hillgrove. They had two boys, Eddie and

Terry, about the same age as my brother Trevor and me. We played all types of games, as four young boys do.

Running by the side of the Hillgrove's house was a railway line with lots of peppercorn trees growing along the sides of the tracks. I can remember us climbing the trees and collecting very large green emperor gum caterpillars, while hanging on for grim death if a train went by, as the tree, the ground and the Hillgrove's house rattled and shook.

I was often told the story of how Mum got to the hospital to give birth to me. Eddie Hillgrove drove her to the Royal Women's in Carlton in his old flat-tray truck. To start it, you needed to slide a crank handle into a hole at the front under the radiator and turn it quickly until the motor kicked over. This was common at the time for most vehicles.

The day I was born, the Second World War was at a very serious stage. On the 8th of June 1944, the Melbourne *Herald* newspaper headline read:

INVASION FORCES CAPTURE BAYEUX

London today – Allied invasion troops have captured the town of BAYEUX, five miles from the English Channel and 18 miles north-west of Caen.

The Allied invasion troops have cleared all landing beaches of the German defenders and in some cases have established links with flanking beach-heads.

My father served in the war, but he was home by this time, having been seriously wounded in 1942. My dad's full name was Ronald William Orton Smith, born 2 January 1918 in Darlford, England. He had two brothers and a sister: Albert, Ivo and Catherine. Dad's father, my grandfather,

Albert Jordan Smith, was also in Australia, and lived not far away, in the rough inner suburbs of Melbourne.

With plenty of family and friends around, our home always seemed busy. Mum and Dad's best and lifelong friends, Betty and Bernie Groom, would often visit. Bernie was also in the army during the war although I'm not sure where he served.

I remember all of the people who were around our home: my grandfather Albert and his partner Rene; Dad's younger brother Ivo, who served in the navy; Mum's youngest sister Josie and her boyfriend Danny, who drove an old car on which the roof folded back on hot days; and Uncle Maurie and his wife May.

Uncle Maurie rode a motorbike with a sidecar, and he often took us kids, all loaded into the sidecar, for rides around the neighbourhood. Nobody wore helmets or had seatbelts and if there were rules about this, we didn't follow them.

This close group of family and friends relied on each other for most things; they would often be at our home for meals that usually became very social occasions. My dad would play the mouth organ, and he and his father played in the Collingwood Mouth Organ Band. There was always lots of noise and singing of old songs and this seemed to me to be what adults did before transistor radios and television.

As a little kid with big ears I often overheard things that probably I shouldn't have. One was about my mum's best friend Betty Groom, whom Mum and my nana talked about performing abortions on Mum's and Betty's friends, usually as a result of having a good time with the American soldiers who were in Melbourne during the war.

Often their talks were about American soldiers and sailors having plenty of money to buy nylon stockings, chocolates and anything else to impress the local girls. I remember clearly that this did not go down well with the husbands and boyfriends who had returned from the war.

I can understand why. Dad joined the Australian Military Forces at the Melbourne Town Hall on the 22nd of June 1940 at just 22 years of age. His Army number was VX34907 and he was assigned to the 2nd/24th Battalion. They were subsequently sent to the Middle East, where the Australians became known as the Rats of Tobruk.

During the battle of El Alamein, on the 26th of October 1942, my dad was wounded by a bullet through his left leg. He was admitted to a tent hospital in Gaza. During this battle, his mates Bluey Beasy and Arthur Chisholm were killed and another friend, Norm Reid, was wounded.

My dad kept a war diary, which I still have.

68th day in hospital, leg swollen but I am feeling fine. Very quiet day very monotonous, old Butch was very drunk.

2nd of January 1943. Golly visited me this evening and brought me a bottle of beer. Much rather be having the bottle with Marg.

This was Dad's twenty-fifth birthday. What a way to spend your birthday, after 68 days in a tent hospital in the middle of a war zone.

It's impossible to comprehend what these young men went through, but certainly possible to understand why they'd take exception to young Americans back home trying to impress their wives and sweethearts.

January the 8th. Told to collect gear to go home, can't believe it to be true.

January 12th. Everyone terribly excited about going home, after so long away it sounds like a dream too good to be true.

January 16th. Left Gaza by train for Suez about 4pm, we crossed the Canal soon after midnight, and it is rather cold in the train. We arrived at Suez about 8am, went out to the ship on a barge had a thrill going up in a sling. Ship left Suez at 4pm. The hospital ship was the HS ORANJE.

January 19th. We have just passed a large group of islands in the Red Sea. Starting to get very warm.

January 20th. Pay day, 3 pounds 20 shillings. We are expected to reach Adelaide Tuesday the 2nd of February.

January the 25th. One of the Aussies on board passed away today, he is to be buried at sea tomorrow.

January the 26th. Burial at sea took place at 5pm in a very calm sea; the coffin wouldn't sink, still floating when we sailed again.

January 30th. Ship told to proceed to New Zealand instead of Adelaide. All Aussies disappointed as we are not far from Aussie. Concert tonight very good.

February 3rd. Pay day, 5 pounds for each year overseas, I drew 10 pounds.

February 5th. Arrived in New Zealand, Kiwis received a great welcome from wives and sweethearts. I felt very envious of them.

February 26th. Arrived in Melbourne lunchtime today, went by private car to Heidelberg Hospital. Met my sweetheart again first time for two-and-a-half years.

As he wrote in his diary, the hospital ship which transported Dad home was the *HS Oranje*. This was its first voyage carrying patients of the British and Allied forces from Suez to Durban in November and December of 1942.

I'm not sure where the following poem is from, but I also found it in my dad's diary.

A poem from abroad, 1942

Thoughts

Thoughts of home and loved ones welfare

Thoughts of town or gum trees tall,

Thoughts of all those things most cherished

Thoughts for which we've offered all.

Thoughts of many Eastern wand'rings,

Fun and war and comrades gone,

Thoughts of tasks that lie before us,

Thoughts to help us carry on.

Now come thoughts of Yuletide greetings,

Couched in terms of love and cheer,

Thoughts of mutual strength and courage,

Thoughts to face the coming year.

Chapter 2:
On the move

When I was about seven, we moved house to St Albans, a new suburb 25 kilometres from Melbourne, where I attended St Albans State School from Grade 2 in 1951 until Grade 6 in 1955.

I remember large open paddocks where my brother and other kids played all sorts of games as varied as our imagination. We'd run ourselves to exhaustion until dark and then go home for dinner. We rode our bikes to school and nearby suburbs, and despite our bikes being second-hand we soon learned to maintain and keep them in good nick with a coat of paint. All through these years I was obsessed with playing Australian Rules Football. My footy was always clean and polished and I can remember taking it to bed on occasions.

On weekends, Dad would take us rabbiting in the nearby hills around Keilor. We had some ferrets and rabbit nets. We'd put the nets at the entrance to the rabbit burrow and the ferret into the burrow to chase the rabbit out and into the net. The rabbits were killed and taken home, where Mum was able to make a variety of meals, adding potatoes, onions, carrots and so on.

Mum was a good cook and able to feed us well, even though we were very poor. We soon learned that if we didn't eat all that was dished up, including cheap vegetables (Brussel sprouts, cabbage, swede, parsnip etc.) we went without.

(These days I feel sick at the thought of a rabbit being killed, let alone actually eating it.)

Our house was in the centre of three identical homes, surrounded by paddocks. Both neighbours were young families; ironically on one side were the Browns, the other side the Jones, with us Smiths in the middle. Mum and Dad became good friends with Kath and Bob Brown. I spent a lot of time with their two kids, Gary and Lorraine. Lorraine was the first girl that I thought of as a girlfriend. We were innocent young kids, but I was smitten at the time.

Dad bought my brother and me a horse. It was a half draught horse, black with a white spot on the forehead and her name was Betsy. (I don't know how Dad afforded a horse; probably better that I didn't know.) We kept Betsy in a nearby paddock and taught ourselves to ride, although I'm not sure how much my brother actually got to ride her.

At about this time I was selling newspapers before school at the St Albans railway station. There were three morning newspapers, the *Sun*, the *Age* and the *Argus*.

I remember selling papers at the station on my tenth birthday. Eventually I was selling the *Herald* after school as well, and delivering morning papers to homes riding my horse. Sometimes Betsy refused to go into a particular street so those customers missed out on their morning news.

One Sunday morning, my brother Trevor and I were riding Betsy home from Sunday School. I was on the front and Trevor was behind, hanging on around my waist. Something spooked Betsy, she bolted and we went galloping along a footpath. There was a man on the path but we had no chance of stopping and crashed into him. Betsy kept going and we hung on until we arrived home.

We didn't know if the man was dead or alive and decided that we wouldn't tell anyone about it. To this day we still don't know how badly the man was injured, if at all. I'm not sure if we ever went back to Sunday School after that episode.

In 1956, I began my secondary education at Sunshine Technical School. I was still obsessed with playing football and any other opportunity to be involved in sport.

I look back now and can't believe how luck would have it that our maths teacher, a weightlifter, had been selected in the upcoming 1956 Olympic Games in Melbourne. His name was Vern Barbaras and he put on a weightlifting exhibition at school.

Through Mr Barbaras I was able to get tickets to attend a few days of the athletics at the Melbourne Cricket Ground. I was inspired by Betty Cuthbert winning a gold medal in the 100 metres, Vladimir Kuts in the distance races, and all of the competitors on the arena.

My new goal was to be an Olympic athlete.

The world was changing rapidly around this time. Television began in time to cover the Olympic Games, although not many people could afford to buy a set. Crowds would gather outside department and electrical goods stores to watch the telecasts. Washing machines, refrigerators, transistor radios, electric ovens and hotplates – things we now take for granted – were being invented and gradually becoming a necessity in the family home. Cars were becoming more common and our daily deliveries of milk and bread (not to mention my own newspaper delivery style on Betsy) gradually changed from horse and cart to purpose-built vans.

Chapter 3:
Country living

At the end of 1956 we moved again, this time to a small country town called Campbells Creek, five kilometres from Castlemaine and 144 kilometres from Melbourne.

I wanted to ride Betsy to Campbells Creek, but my parents weren't happy about that so we had to sell her.

My dad had secured a job in Castlemaine at Thompsons Foundry, a large manufacturer of train wheels for the state government, amongst other things.

Campbells Creek was a small goldfield town. Gold was discovered in 1851 and within two years 3000 miners were living in a shantytown stretching along the creek. A makeshift village served by the obligatory chain of hotels, a brewery, two churches and a chapel school were the only things there.

Our home in Campbells Creek was a tiny house made from concrete. We had to burn wood in an oven to cook, heat water and warm the house. Campbells Creek in 1956 consisted of a general store, post office, hotel, football ground, outdoor swimming pool, a Mechanics Hall and a state school.

I have fond memories of this time. My grandfather, Albert, would often stay with us and he and I would wake up early and go for serious walks. Albert still lived in inner suburban Melbourne, but loved visiting us in the 'country'. I remember he walked with a very straight back and strode out with military precision. He included push-ups and stretching in his exercise 'routine' and, looking back, these were probably my first formal workouts.

I'd always been very active, running, riding my bike, playing football, cricket, all sorts of games and activities, but had never thought of exercise just to be fit.

My grandfather was a very proud and righteous man. I don't think that he drank alcohol and he may have been religious, which were highly unusual traits in our immediate family. Despite our poverty Mum and Dad seemed to drink to excess.

My memories of my childhood are mostly of happy times. That's why I've never really been able to understand why my brother Trevor and his wife to this day blame his many years of depression on his childhood.

It's interesting how different siblings have different interpretations. Although there were some terrible times, for me it was mostly fun.

Over the years my brother and his wife have constantly brought up times when the three of us kids (my brother, sister and me) were locked inside the family car while Mum and Dad were drinking inside a hotel. (I don't think children were allowed inside hotels in those days.)

I clearly remember our hair-raising drives from our home in Campbells Creek to my auntie and uncle's housing commission house in Braybrook, a suburb nine kilometres west of Melbourne and a 140-kilometre drive from Campbells Creek. My dad drove a Ford mainline ute, blue, with a bench seat that somehow the five of us were able to fit across. There were no such things as seatbelts.

These early days growing up were spent watching the adults drinking, singing, dancing and mainly having a good time. However, I also remember times when my Dad and Mum would scream at each other, probably after having too much to drink, and the more they argued the faster my dad would drive. On at least one occasion I remember we were travelling at 100 miles per hour, that's 160 kilometres, on very narrow roads on our way home. I remember Mum getting out when Dad stopped on one of our trips home and Dad drove off, with us three kids screaming in the car. Mum arrived the next day after hitchhiking home.

This type of behaviour, unfortunately, was quite common growing up and it astounds me how we, as humans, are able to adapt to our environment and in our minds, even as children, can normalise these circumstances.

To make matters worse, it was common for Mum to have male friends at our home, who were usually introduced as 'uncles'. Seeing my mother in compromising situations with different men is something I've never discussed with anybody.

The last time I remember this behaviour was one night after Zandra (my first wife) and I were married and living in Bolton Street, between Eltham and Montmorency. Mum was banging on our door and so I let her and her friend inside; they'd been drinking and arguing. He was a well-known VFL (now known as AFL) footballer. And this was all going on while my dad was either working or at home, with no knowledge of this behaviour.

To me, Campbells Creek was paradise; rolling hills of farmland, thick bush nearby and a creek at the back of our house where we fished and occasionally caught redfin and yabbies. We learned very quickly, while exploring the overgrown Chinese cemeteries in the bush, that deep, dangerous overgrown holes (mine shafts) were scattered throughout the area.

We panned for specks of gold close to the small town of Chewton, four kilometres south-east of Castlemaine. Chewton is a charming old gold mining town on the Pyrenees Highway in the Victorian Central Highlands. The main mine still operates, making it one of the country's longest running gold mining endeavours.

Trevor and I would ride our bikes on these adventures, often sleeping in the bush overnight, having packed a bag with tinned sausage and vegetables, baked beans, biscuits or anything else we could scrounge from home.

On one side of our house was a lemonade factory and the property on the other side was a large horseracing establishment belonging to the Ford family, a racing dynasty in country Victoria. The owner of this property was Poe Ford, an unforgettable character and legend in the area. It wasn't long before he and I were buddies – a 12-year-old and (what I remember as) a grumpy old man.

I loved helping Poe with the horses and all of the chores that go with training racehorses. He spent a lot of time teaching me to ride properly. Once Poe was happy with my horseriding ability, it was common for him and me to load up two horses in the float behind his truck, just after 4.00 on a Tuesday and Thursday morning, and drive to Bendigo racecourse, 40 kilometres away, where I'd ride track work. Then Poe would drive home and I'd go off to Castlemaine Technical School, where athletics and football were my fondest activities.

During Melbourne Cup time in 1957, Poe told me that he thought a horse called Straight Draw would win the Cup. So the day before the Cup, I started to take bets at school.

I told the kids that I'd been given a tip; of course, the horse I said could win was not the horse Poe told me would win. Straight Draw won the race; I cleaned up and thought I was a very smart little 13-year-old.

But the longer I was involved in horseracing, the more I learned not to trust anyone.

Across the road from our home was a small fruit and vegetable shop run by a husband and wife. I helped out in the shop after school and kept the owner company on his weekly trips to Queen Victoria Market in Melbourne. We'd leave the shop around midnight and drive his old truck the 140 kilometres to the market. I can remember the hustle and bustle of this busy place in the early hours of the morning, with traders of all nationalities haggling over prices for fruit and vegetables. I'm sure I learned more valuable life skills there at the market than from anything I was ever taught at school. The shop owner would then drive back home, while I probably slept most of the way back.

Living in a small country town was a unique experience. We didn't own a television set, so it was up to us kids to keep ourselves occupied.

The local Mechanics Hall was the place where all things happened. I tried learning the bagpipes and drums there, as the local Scottish band practiced in the hall, but I soon realised that music and I were poles apart.

By this time I'd become obsessed with racehorses, helping Poe take horses to the track, where I listened and learned as much as I could about being a part of the team of strappers, jockeys, owners and the whole racing industry.

Chapter 4:
Go ride a horse

By the end of 1957 I talked my parents into letting me leave school. I was 13 years and six months old. Poe had contacts in the racing industry and got me a job in a horseracing stable near the racetrack in Caulfield. The stable was owned by Charlie Sanderson, a leading horse trainer in Melbourne. Charlie's son was also called Charlie and was a leading jumps jockey; he also rode in England during the jumping season.

This was a big thing for me, as my parents still lived in Campbells Creek and I was living in a small room under the same roof as the horses.

I soon learned that it was a tough life starting at the bottom of the system, not knowing anybody, starting work in the early morning dark preparing horses to go to the track, which involved grooming and putting on bridles and saddles. Charlie would ride his pony and lead two horses and I would ride one horse and lead another. This was challenging in itself because we had to go over a busy rail crossing and through traffic to reach the Caulfield racecourse training area.

As a young, new and probably not very good rider, I was only allowed to ride the not-so-good racehorses. The good horses were ridden by the best jockeys. I thought it strange that the good horses were usually well behaved, whereas the not-so-good ones had minds of their own.

It was a thrill for me to mix with some of the best jockeys in the land. I watched the champion horse Tulloch, ridden by George Moore, working out. Tulloch's muscles were magnificent, shining with sweat, as steam rose off this amazing animal at the end of the workout.

I enjoyed race days, when we'd load the horses into a large transport truck. The strappers would travel in the truck with the horses to the various racetracks. Looking after horses before and after they raced was intense, as the trainers, owners and jockeys always seemed on edge, except after a win.

My plan was to become an apprentice jockey so I began studies at the apprentice school at Caulfield Racecourse, although over time it was obvious to me and others that I was going to be too heavy to be a jockey.

By this time my parents had obtained a war service loan and were able to buy a new two-bedroom weatherboard house at 55 Adam Crescent, Montmorency. This was to be their last home, after all the years of moving from house to house. I left the stables and moved back with my parents.

My dad got me a job as an apprentice fitter and turner, which was a five-year commitment at a company called Mindrill, a general engineering firm that made mining exploration drilling equipment and machinery, converting ex-war service army trucks into mobile drilling rigs. It was a good job and I attended school one day a week, initially at Preston Technical College and for the last two years at the Royal Melbourne Institute of Technology.

As luck would have it, one of the tradesmen that worked for the company was a part-time trainer. His name was Jack Smith (no relation), we soon hit it off and I began to ride track work for him.

Eventually, despite worries about my size, I did qualify as an amateur jockey and was able to ride in what were then referred to as picnic races. These had a minimum riding weight of nine stone seven pounds or 60 kilograms and I was able to ride at this weight quite comfortably. Picnic race meets were held in country towns around Victoria like Healesville, Yarra Glen, Yea and Wesburn. I loved the country races and learned a lot about life from people in the racing industry over these years.

Some of the valuable lessons were obvious. One was to mind your own business, keep your mouth shut unless you were asked and, most importantly, watch out for yourself. Because when money was involved, people from all walks of life, some good and some not so good, weren't always on the right side of the law.

Away from work and horseracing, I started to hang around the streets of Eltham with older boys and make some poor choices about life in general. I thought hanging out with this group was the cool thing to do, even when we broke into several shops in Eltham's Main Street and also a small lock-up at the Eltham Football Club. I was silly enough to make a small jemmy bar at work, to enable us to remove some boards from the shop at the club rooms.

Two of the other boys had stolen cars before this, and probably done other and worse things of which I was unaware.

Well, as a result, the police arrived at my parents' house and took my dad and me to the Eltham Police Station, where I made a statement about the series of events in which I was involved and went home with my dad, after being told that I would have to appear at Eltham Court on a certain date.

This was a terrible shock to my mum and dad as they had no idea what I'd been up to. I'd always been a good hardworking kid. I'm sure at the time it broke their hearts.

My dad and I went to court on the appointed day. I was under 16 so this was the Children's Court. Fortunately, I was placed on a good behaviour bond. Two of the older boys went to prison. Another, who was interviewed first by the police and had given details of what had been going on, was later killed in a car crash.

My probation officer was a man called George Newton, an unarmed combat instructor with the Australian Army. Part of the probation guidelines were that I regularly attend the local police Youth Boys Club. This was a turning point in my life and possibly the best thing that ever happened to me.

Chapter 5:
The (young) boxer

George Newton was an instructor at the local Youth Boys Club. He taught boxing, wrestling and judo. He appeared to me to be the fittest, toughest person I had ever met.

Although I was initially quite scared of him, I had enormous respect for the work that he did for young people and the community. He took me under his wing and I seemed to pick up the skills of boxing quickly. In hindsight, possibly my years of riding racehorses helped, as I was strong and lean, with a high power-to-weight ratio.

I had my first novice boxing match just three weeks after starting at the boys club, at the football club rooms in nearby Diamond Creek. A group of boys from the club competed and I was lucky enough to win my bout against another novice boy.

I was on my way again, now with a new obsession to learn all I could about boxing. I was very lucky, as some of the older volunteers at the club had a lot of experience. I think I was smart enough to listen to all they could tell and demonstrate. They were terrific people, who had grown up in very tough times.

This, together with George and his positive attitude, taught me that if you work harder than everybody else almost anything is possible.

I trained every day, running of a morning before work usually three miles (5 km) and then to the club each weeknight, where training included skipping, sparring, boxing skill sessions, medicine ball, dumbbells, grappling, wrestling and anything else that George could make up. One of his favourite drills was to have me lie on the floor, his feet either side of me, while he would throw a large leather medicine ball onto my stomach up to 100 times.

George would drive me one night a week to a boxing gym in Preston, run by a well-known professional boxing trainer, Sid "Snowy" Thompson. I was able to spar in a boxing ring with a variety of opponents, including some experienced, professional boxers. Of a weekend, my training continued with a variety of activities like running through local bush tracks, chopping wood for George at his property, and a skipping routine in the kitchen at home where my sister would time me with a stop watch. I'd skip 15 three-minute rounds with a minute break between rounds.

I continued to compete in boxing tournaments around Victoria, usually held in halls in rural towns such as Bendigo, Benalla or Maffra, and run by the local police Youth Boys Club.

At 16 years of age, in 1960, I competed in the Victorian Boxing Championships run by the Victorian Amateur Boxing Association, winning all of my bouts to become the junior amateur flyweight champion of Victoria.

These tournaments were run every year as a knockout competition. Entrants in each weight division would compete against each other until the last two fought for the title.

The boy that I boxed in the final was Arthur Thomas, an aboriginal boy from Gippsland, who later became a very successful professional boxer. In later years he boxed in the main event on the first episode of *TV Ringside* on Channel 7 in Melbourne.

Over the next few years I continued to play under-age football with Eltham, and still rode the occasional horserace for Jack Smith – but I was obsessed with becoming the best boxer that I could be.

With the help of my mum I wrote to Percy Cerutty asking his advice on fitness training. Fifty years ago Percy Wells Cerutty was a man before his time – a prophet in the realm of human endeavour. He was regarded as an eccentric by many, but his philosophy of fitness still stands the test of time.

In those days he was training a group of athletes at his camp in Portsea on the Mornington Peninsula in Victoria. Three of these athletes were Herb Elliot, Ron Clark and John Landy, who all went on to become some of Australia's greatest performers.

Percy's view on diet, as on most things, was strict and uncompromising. Raw, unrefined and unprocessed was how Cerutty liked his food. The basis of his diet included rolled oats, dried fruits, fruit, vegetables, fish, water (litres each day), milk, nuts and a little meat.

Percy kindly wrote back with some fitness advice specifically for me, for which I am forever grateful. I always wished that I could have spent time at his training camp.

I continued boxing in Victoria and New South Wales country towns such as Griffith, Leeton and around the suburbs of Melbourne, including Dandenong, Collingwood and Footscray.

In 1961 I won the senior amateur flyweight Victorian championships. Then in 1962 I won the senior amateur bantamweight title.

Later in 1962 I travelled to Sydney by train as part of the Victorian Boxing Team to compete in the elimination trials for the upcoming Commonwealth Games in Perth. This was an exciting trip for a young, innocent 18-year-old. The team coach was Leo Berry, a leading boxing trainer from Richmond, and others on the team included Bob Dolby and Brendan McMahon, who were to become leading professional boxers.

Along with some of the team from NSW we were shown the sights of Sydney, including the seedy side of Kings Cross, where we were taken along some narrow laneways with lots of doorways and windows. In every one of them was a prostitute wearing very little. I remember vividly that they all seemed to have enormous boobs. The area was packed with people walking up and down and I was terrified that one of the others would try to talk me into going with one of these women. I was so glad that didn't happen. I was nervous, self-conscious and glad to get out of there without being embarrassed any further.

My opponent in my first fight of the tournament was Jeffrey "Mitta" Dynevor. I'd never heard of him; he was an Aboriginal man 32 years old and bantamweight champion of Queensland. I soon learned that he was a skilled, powerful boxer. I was totally overwhelmed and the bout was stopped in the first round.

Mitta went on to win a gold medal in the Commonwealth Games and became the first Aboriginal person to win a gold medal in any Commonwealth or Olympic Games. He remains the only Aboriginal person to ever win a gold medal for boxing. Before the Games, he'd even beaten Lionel Rose. A few years later Lionel would win the bantamweight championship of the world and go on to become one of the best boxers Australia ever produced.

Looking back, I was completely shattered and extremely disappointed in my effort but, with hindsight, I'm glad it turned out the way it did. I'm sure that the humbling experience has helped me in the long term to remain grounded and not get ahead of myself.

Chapter 6:
And the young husband

At about 16 years of age, Zandra Lecher and I became boyfriend and girlfriend.

We lived about half a kilometre apart and were typical young kids, innocent and immature. I was working as an apprentice fitter and turner at Mindrill in nearby Preston, and totally absorbed with my boxing. Zandra worked part time in a cake shop in Eltham and was dedicated to ballet dancing. Her brother Ray and sister Cheryl were like a younger brother and sister to me. Zandra's parents, Jack and Alma, were heavy drinkers like my mum and dad, and regular patrons of the Eltham Hotel. Jack was a real estate agent with a shop beside the Eltham railway station.

I remember family holidays with the Lechers as very special and, interestingly, I don't remember ever having a holiday with my own family. One of these holidays was camping on the foreshore of the Point Leo Surf Beach on the Mornington Peninsula; another was at a holiday house in Tootgarook. I remember Zandra and I going to a rock'n'roll dance in a hall at Tootgarook. Zandra, in an attempt to rebel, dyed her hair green. Well, it was the sixties!

We occasionally went to rock'n'roll dances at the Preston Town Hall. This was the venue where leading bands would play in suburban Melbourne. Some of the most popular groups and bands of the time were Johnny

Chester and the Chessmen, Col Joye and the Joy Boys, and Normie Rowe and his band. These groups were also regulars on the popular TV shows, Johnny O'Keefe's *Six O'clock Rock* and Brian Henderson's *Bandstand*.

The world was a different place all those years ago. Alcohol and drugs were never even thought of at places like this.

Zandra and I often thought of building our own house at the back of her parents' large block, behind their home. Looking back, we were so young and naive.

In September 1962 we became engaged; I was 18 and Zandra was 17 years old. My dad told me it was a stupid idea – we were too young and didn't know what we were doing. Being a smart-arsed 18-year-old, I thought I knew better and told him that he didn't know what he was talking about.

In September 1963 we were married, with Zandra four months pregnant, and in February 1964 our beautiful daughter Sheree was born in the Greensborough Hospital. We went on to have two more lovely daughters, Kelly and Debbie.

Our first house was a little weatherboard between Eltham and Montmorency; after a few years we bought a new house in Diamond Creek.

By this time I'd finished my apprenticeship with Mindrill and had a new job as a tradesman at Lovett Tools in Para Road, Greensborough. To help buy our new house I was also working part time at the Diamond Creek Hotel as a barman – and often as a bouncer. I was also training and boxing. Working two jobs, being a husband, father and athlete, I realise now I probably didn't do any of them very well or to the best of my ability.

My boxing continued during 1963 and 1964, where most of my fitness training was done running around the country roads of Diamond Creek, at a private gym in Eltham that George Newton had access to and sparring at Snowy Thompson's gym, which had now moved to Brunswick.

I continued to be quite successful; my goal was to win selection for the 1964 Tokyo Olympic Games. The final selection trials were held in the Channel 9 studios in Melbourne on a Sunday afternoon. The show was hosted by Maurie and Wayne Kirby and the refercc was Gus Mercurio. I was now in the featherweight division (less than 57 kg) and came up against the Queenslander Randall Hope. It was a close fight but Randall got the decision and was off to Tokyo. As second-placegetter I received a pair of Aquila shoes, much to my utter dismay, and still to this day have a chuckle when I see Aquila shoes anywhere.

I was extremely disappointed and made the decision to give professional boxing a try. But over the next two or three years, both my boxing and my marriage didn't work out as I had hoped – probably due to my lack of passion and effort, always taking the easy approach and assuming a half-hearted effort was good enough.

I'd started drinking and although I was still training with George Newton and Sid Thompson and sparring in the Brunswick gym, now even against leading professional boxers, I really didn't have my heart in it. These boxers included Ben Brizzi, Billy Murphy and Hilary Connelly.

George was also taking me to Leo Berry's gym in Richmond, a rundown council-owned property and part of the local swimming pool complex. However, it was always busy, as the international boxers competing at Melbourne's Festival Hall would work out against local boxers to prepare for their upcoming bouts. I was fortunate to spar with some of these internationals, one of them a black American named Don Johnston. He taught me so much in these sessions. He was known as "Gentleman Don" and he certainly proved that to me.

Don Johnston fought against John Famechon in 1967, Jose Legra also in 1967 and Lionel Rose in 1970, three of the best featherweights in the history of world boxing.

Berry's gym was also a place that attracted well-known underworld identities. I soon learned that if you treated people with respect, minded your own business, heard nothing and said nothing, there'd be no problems. One day I was getting changed in the dilapidated change rooms while two notorious characters got into their workout gear. Each had a pistol in a pouch around their chest, which they casually removed, hung in their locker with their clothes and, of course, nothing was said by anybody.

My professional boxing career progressed in stops and starts, just as my life seemed to be progressing all over the place. I had 18 fights over about three years, some at Festival Hall in Melbourne, others in regional towns and a few on Channel 7 at the studio in Dorcas Street, South Melbourne. I won about half my 18 bouts.

I remain disappointed that I didn't achieve the results that I believe I had the potential to achieve.

I know now that all success in life comes from hard work, passion and being true to yourself. What you put in is what you get out. Success in boxing encompasses the whole package – good nutrition, solid, regular, consistent training, no alcohol, self-belief and being honest with yourself and those around you.

Chapter 7:
Breakups and breakdowns

After five or six years my marriage had completely broken down, and Zandra and I had separated. I'm not sure how or when, as my brain has blocked out most of my young married life. I suspect that leaving my children, years of heavy drinking and feeling sorry for myself, and massive guilt all contributed to my poor subconscious coping mechanisms.

During the next stage of my life, I worked in a factory in West Heidelberg, W&D Engineering. It was a good job. We made conveyor systems for high-speed packaging and stacking systems, which we would then install and commission in places such as breweries and food production companies.

I also had a part-time job at night and weekends at the Templestowe Hotel, an outer eastern suburb of Melbourne, and it was there that I met June Sadler. She would have a night out with a group of friends, usually once a week, and we connected quickly. June was engaged and I was married (although separated) and we became friends and spent time together, usually with her friend Olga.

June broke off her engagement, much to the disappointment of her family, and I'm sure they hated me from the start. We spent as much time as we could together, but we were both working and she was still living at her parents' home in Surrey Hills. They had forbidden her from seeing me, so most of our time together was still spent with her friend Olga.

I'd bought myself a Volkswagen Kombi van fitted with a table, bench, fridge, bed and so on and had become a bit of a gypsy.

One night, after working late at the Templestowe Hotel and probably drinking too much, I was driving to Mum's house in Montmorency when I ran off the side of the road and rolled down an embankment. I wasn't hurt and, when the tow truck had dragged my Kombi back onto the road, I completed the drive to Mum's. I rang June at her parents and her father answered, not happy that I'd rung so late. He told me never to ring or contact her again, and he never told June that I'd called.

The next time I caught up with June we had a long discussion and decided to go away together. We had a plan and a week or so later June left her parents a note and we were off.

Initially, we drove to Mildura on the NSW border where we lived in the Kombi in a caravan park and worked picking oranges and any other available jobs. We gradually worked our way across the Nullarbor Plain. In those days most of the road was dirt, hot and dusty, but eventually we arrived in Perth. We found a flat to rent in Wembley, an inner suburb, and to us it was paradise after our time on the road and the tired caravan parks we'd camped in along the way.

I soon found a job in an engineering factory close by and started playing football again; life was good but we were very short of money.

Things got tougher when during a football match my leg got caught in a scramble of players and I was taken by ambulance to the Royal Perth Hospital. I had an operation on my right knee and two medial cartilages were removed. I woke up with my leg in plaster from the ankle to above the knee; the cast was supposed to stay on for four months.

Because of this injury I lost my job and we struggled to pay the rent. I soon removed the plaster from my leg myself so that I could get back to work.

Chapter 8:
Heat in the Pilbara

I applied for a job as an installation fitter tradesman at the Perth office of Dravo Pty Ltd. The site was the construction of the Robe River crushing and pelletising plant at Cape Lambert in Western Australia, 1550 kilometres from Perth.

Off we went on the next leg of our adventure into the unknown. The road north was mostly dirt, baking hot and unforgiving, and we soon learned the importance of carrying plenty of drinking water, as the Kombi was having problems. With absolutely nothing between small towns it was vital we had enough food and water to see us through.

We arrived at Cape Lambert and I began the job. The size of this project was mind-blowing, with 3000 employees living in single men's quarters. We were fortunate enough to rent a 22-foot caravan with air conditioning and an annexe in a caravan park in a nearby town called Roebourne.

Roebourne is a former gold rush town 202 kilometres from Port Headland and 1563 kilometres from Perth in the WA Pilbara region, which prospered during the gold boom of the late 19th century. At the time we were there, the town consisted of a hotel, caravan sales and service centre, general store, post office and caravan park. June was lucky, and scored a job at the caravan business. Most of the local people were Aboriginal and lived close by in various outback locations.

There were about 10 families in the caravan park who worked on the project, and we'd travel on a company bus to and from the site each day, usually between 10 and 20 kilometres, depending where we were working that particular day. The work was hot and hard, but the company provided everything it could to ensure the employees were cared for under the extreme conditions. The food in the mess rooms was substantial, with lots of it; drums of iced water were positioned around the work sites, along with salt tablets.

The actual project was known as the Robe River Pelletising Plant, and it began with the construction of a rail line. This railway originally linked the joint venture's first mine, near Pannawonica in the Robe River valley, with a pelletising plant and port at Cape Lambert.

The length of this section of rail line was 160 kilometres. The Rio Tinto iron ore train consisted of up to 236 wagons, each with a load capacity of up to 106 tons. Trains were up to 2.4 kilometres long and fully loaded weighed 29,500 tons.

At the end of the rail line a crushing plant was constructed. A series of conveyors transported the iron ore dust to enormous rotating drums that rolled the iron ore into small balls (the size of a marble) where they were fed onto more conveyors and transferred onto a newly constructed wharf and, finally, onto Japanese cargo ships to be taken to Japan and turned into steel.

Life was hard but satisfying and I was making good money. We gradually got out of debt and even saved some money at last. The caravan community was a close-knit group, as life was demanding. The temperature in the van annexe on one occasion reached 52 degrees. Another time we had to tie everything down securely as a cyclone hit the coast close by. Fortunately we weren't injured and had no serious damage, but at the time it was frightening.

One Sunday on our day off June and I drove to an isolated part of this amazing coastline to go fishing. We drove over a rocky beach that appeared to be solid ground, but when we returned to our faithful Kombi, the back wheels had sunk into the stones and we were bogged. We tried to dig the rear wheels free and drive forward but it only made things worse. We realised that we were in a serious situation. We had very little water, the Kombi didn't have a radiator as an emergency water supply, the motor of the Kombi was in the rear end and was very heavy, causing the car to sink to the axle, we had no communication, it was extremely hot and we would certainly perish if we didn't find a solution.

In a state of knowing that we could both die, somehow I managed to lift the rear of the Kombi as June planted her foot. Incredibly, she made it forward far enough to find stable ground. When we got back to the caravan park a group of us tried to lift the rear end of the Kombi and discovered it just wasn't possible. Somehow in that extreme situation, I was able to do the impossible.

It wasn't long after this incident that our trusty Kombi died. We bought a Ford Falcon from the caravan dealership where June worked. One night, a group of couples from the caravan park went to an outdoor movie night at the camp where the single men were housed. This caused such a disruption when we walked in with the women, with men screaming and totally out of control, that we had to abandon the idea and get out of there quick smart.

Work was going well and I was promoted from an installation fitter to a leading hand and then foreman until the end of the construction phase of this massive project. I was part of a small group of the management team that helped with the plant's commissioning. Towards the end of this new job, June and I decided to try to have a baby, so she stopped taking the pill.

When the project wound up in the Pilbara, we took off on the long journey back to Perth and then across the Nullarbor to Melbourne.

Our plans to start a family had worked. June was pregnant and we had a difficult trip, with car problems and the relentless heat and dust on this long, lonely stretch of road.

Chapter 9:
Goodbyes and beginnings

In 1972, Dad died after a long and tough battle with cancer. When I reflect on his life he was a terrific dad. After being wounded in the war he walked with a limp and at times used a walking stick. My fondest memories are of him teaching me to kick a football with both feet, and building a boxing ring in the backyard and teaching me to box. He also built a high jump frame as I had won the high jump at the school sports and went on to compete with the Castlemaine Harriers Athletic Club. I don't know how, as we never seemed to have any money, but it didn't stop him buying what was needed for me to participate. I remember him having me fitted for running spikes at a sports store in Footscray; the salesman was Jack Collins, a famous full forward with the Footscray Football Club.

My sporting ability obviously came from Dad's side of the family, although he never talked about it. His mates often told me stories of him being a tough competitor, and about his bravery and courage both before and after being wounded in the Middle East.

Dad's sister Catherine had a daughter named Dale who was a champion sprinter and narrowly missed Olympic selection in the late sixties and seventies. Other members on the Smith side of the family also had some sporting ability; Trevor was a very good boxer as well, and his youngest son Bradley a very successful long-distance runner. I don't remember Mum's side of the family having any athletic ability at all.

My dad was a very quiet and gentle man who openly showed emotion and empathy to others. He loved and was very close to his first grandchild Sheree, my first daughter.

I feel so much guilt for the fact that I was a pain in the arse to my dad and not very nice to him on many occasions.

I thought that I knew everything and he knew nothing about life. I now know how wrong and what a dickhead I was. I would give anything to be able to spend one minute with him, to not only apologise but give him the opportunity to see that at long last I've grown up and am trying to make a difference to a world that he fought so hard to protect for all of us.

To this day I still harbour an enormous amount of guilt and regret over my dad and just hope I can find some peace someday.

My place of solace since 2009 has been my boxing gym. Along one end hang seven heavy punching bags. Several times, when I've been in the gym by myself contemplating life, cleaning up or having a coffee in the still of the early morning or last thing at night and, even though there has been no wind, one of the punching bags has begun to rock back and forth. I'm convinced that my dad is around me, checking that I'm OK. I feel his presence strongly.

After arriving back in Melbourne we rented a small flat in Caulfield. June caught up with her parents but I was never welcome and it put June in a difficult position. We got on with our lives the best we could.

I initially worked as a labourer for a builder who was a long-time friend. One of the big projects we worked on was in Mt Eliza, a very upmarket but small village on the

Mornington Peninsula. I never in my wildest dreams would have thought that in years to come Mt Eliza would be my home.

I decided to get a 'real' job and in January 1973 began what was to become a 16-year tenure with Elevators Pty Ltd. I was employed as a leading hand fitter. Elevators was an Australian-owned (Lend Lease Corporation) lift company. In 1974 I was promoted to staff foreman and was responsible for the installation of lifts and escalators during the construction of many of Melbourne's high-rise buildings, including Nauru House, Collins Place, State Bank Centre, Ansett House and 505 Little Collins Street. Many of these buildings were constructed with Lend Lease project management systems. At peak construction times I held responsibility for up to 200 employees and had to manage industrial relations, construction programming and costs. I met with building companies and project management teams to discuss features of planning works and so on.

It was indeed a real job, but that didn't mean life was without other difficult challenges.

Chapter 10:
A haunting decision

In February 1973, our beautiful daughter Megan Anne was born at Bethlehem Hospital, Caulfield. June and I were so excited and felt that our life was complete, as do all young parents. We moved to a larger unit in Heathmont, 24 kilometres east of Melbourne. Life was good after living like gypsies for the last couple of years; June was happy as a full-time mum where she had lots of friends and loved making clothes for Megan.

One Sunday, when Megan was 16 months old, the three of us had a day at the zoo. June was a bit wheezy with her long-term asthma. We discussed whether I would go to work the next day or take her to the doctor, and decided that I would go to work and organise her mum to take her to the doctor.

That decision still haunts me.

The next morning, Monday, I travelled to work in the city by train. I walked along Exhibition Street, as usual, just before 7.00, and rang June from a public phone at the corner of Flinders Lane. She said she was fine and that her mother was going to pick her and Megan up and take them to the family doctor. I had a very weird feeling about it but I went off to work.

Later that morning I was called to the site office on the Collins Place construction project to receive a phone call. It was June's sister Margaret. She told me that their mother had taken June to the doctor's rooms and the doctor had given her an injection for her asthma. Then they returned to her mother's home in Surrey Hills. June went to the bathroom, had a respiratory arrest and passed away.

I went by taxi from the city to June's parents' home but by this time her body had gone and I wasn't able to get any further details of her death.

This was a situation I just could not comprehend. It was a living nightmare. June was dead, and the Sadler family didn't want anything to do with me. I was told by June's brother that the family solicitors were looking into the legal guardianship of Megan.

In my head it was very simple – June and I were living as husband and wife and Megan was our daughter.

The day of the funeral my family, friends and work colleagues were all there, but the Sadler family had totally taken over; neither Megan nor I were mentioned. This was confusing to my friends and workmates, as although June and I weren't legally married, most people thought that we were.

Over a period of time and many confrontations with June's sister, I took Megan and moved in with my mum. This wasn't ideal, as although Mum loved Megan, she was old, unwell and drank and smoked far too much.

I was working in the city, leaving home early in the morning and getting back late. I was also drinking a lot and feeling very sorry for myself. Over the next year or so I tried a few different arrangements. At one stage I was dropping Megan off at a friend of June's on my way to work. Sue had two boys and did her best with Megan, but it was all far from perfect.

I was fortunate that my work with Elevators was a constant in my life, although I had some highs and lows.

On one occasion, while working on the construction of a 52-storey building in Exhibition Street, I was involved in a fatal accident in which a father of six was killed. It was a complex situation where two large Favco tower cranes mounted on the top of the building were raising a lift machine room and lift car to a new position in the lift shaft. The lift support cables came free, crashing down onto the roof of the machine room where the crane dogman and I were standing. I was able to jump out of a hole (called a penetration) on the sixteenth floor, but my workmate was killed. I was lucky to escape with minor injuries. I struggled psychologically with this incident as I still believe the accident was avoidable. I'd questioned with management the system of work to carry out this operation before the incident and was overruled.

My personal life by this time had spiralled out of control; I was drinking before work, usually at a hotel in Melbourne that opened at 6am, and also lunchtimes and after work.

This led to socialising with groups of undesirable people, both men and women. One such person was a German man around 30 years of age named Horst. Initially, I was naive with our friendship as he was a lot of fun. It wasn't long before I realised that I was becoming his 'security' as he was buying and selling drugs.

Drugs were something I'd never been exposed to, or knew anything about before this. One night, Horst and I were at the Burvale Hotel in Nunawading, an eastern suburb of Melbourne, where the now-famous band AC/DC was playing. Horst convinced me to take a tiny white pill. I was probably quite drunk and discovered what I had actually taken was LSD. Before long, I was terrified, hallucinating, sweating and holding onto my chair, as

40

everyone in the club appeared to be skeletons dancing around me and the music seemed abnormally loud. I obviously survived that night although I have no recollection of how or when I arrived home. This was the one and only time that I ever took anything like this.

Another episode with Horst was the last Sunbury Pop Festival in January 1975, an annual Australian rock music festival held at George Duncan's Farm in Sunbury, 30 kilometres north-west of Melbourne. It was modelled on "The Woodstock Spirit of Peace and Love". The headline group was Deep Purple; the support bands were up-and-coming Australian groups including Daddy Cool, Sky Hooks, Billy Thorpe and AC/DC. The music played 24 hours a day for three days, the weather was intensely hot, and the place was packed with young people, nudity, noise, beer and drugs.

Horst and I had a small tent that soon became a place where people could buy marijuana. I remember lots of young people, tired and upset by the effects of all this craziness. It wasn't long afterwards that I heard Horst had been deported back to Germany.

Soon after, I met a woman named Ann; she had a daughter a bit older than Megan and after a while we moved in together. I think I hoped that it would work and life would become a bit more normal, as we were able to drop both girls at a child-minding place in St Kilda on our way to work. There were times when this relationship was good; deep down, though, I was concerned about the long-term prospects, as we weren't really good for each other. We drank too much and Ann had a terrible temper. One day, she smacked Megan for some reason, and I decided to pack up and take Megan back to Mum's.

I talked to Mum about Megan's long-term future and we decided to talk to my sister, Glenda. Glenda was married to Alan Paterson and they were unable to have children of their own; they had adopted a baby boy, Martin, who was the same age as Megan, and were hoping to adopt another child.

I met with Glenda and Alan and talked about the best options long term for Megan. I knew the current situation wasn't in my daughter's best interest. In truth, I was deeply ashamed of myself for getting into this situation. I felt that I'd let June down and perhaps Megan would have been better off staying with June's family.

After some thinking time I again met with Glenda and Alan. We agreed that they would adopt Megan. Mum and I thought it was the best option to ensure that Megan could have a normal family childhood.

Looking back now, I'm not sure it was the best idea. At the time it seemed wise.

I continued my relationship with Ann, which was an on-and-off and mostly fiery affair. At times it was good, but in the long term it wasn't. We both had baggage. She'd lived her adult life flirting with and controlling men, and although she wanted us to get married I didn't trust her when she was drinking. That was most days.

I started playing football again, and organised a social competition between a few companies involved in high-rise construction. It was during a social match between Elevators and the Johns & Waygood lift company that I injured my knee again.

Ann drove me to the Alfred Hospital in Prahran, an inner suburb of Melbourne, where I was admitted for further surgery. It would be another turning point in my life.

Chapter 11:
Sharyn Strong

It was the first week of May 1976 when an 18-year-old first-year nurse admitted me to Ward 23 of the Alfred Hospital. Her name was Sharyn Strong.

I was diagnosed as needing a meniscectomy, to remove cartilage from my right knee. I had the surgery and was in hospital for two weeks. During this time Sharyn and I talked a lot and she did her first case study on me as part of her nurse training – assuming that my knee operation was the extent of my medical problems. She would eventually find out about all of my excess baggage, psychological issues, drinking problems, my four kids and some of the other issues in my life. She gave me her parents' home telephone number and told me I could ring if I wanted to talk to someone, even though she didn't live there (she was living in the nurses' hostel in Punt Road, Prahran).

Little did we know that, 41 years later, Sharyn would be my wife, mother of our two kids, my soulmate and best friend.

When I was discharged from hospital I headed to the nearest hotel on my crutches. That night back at our house in Brighton, Ann and I had a big fight. I left, with a wicker washing basket full of clothes and a guitar. That was all I owned in the world. A sorry state of affairs for a man my age. That was the last time I saw Ann.

I had Sharyn's parents' phone number in my wallet so I rang her home (there were no mobile phones in those days).

Her dad answered but had no idea who I was or why I would be trying to contact Sharyn. He knew that Sharyn was at a friend's restaurant in Malvern, with her friends, so he rang the restaurant and told her that some bloke called Ron had rung and wanted to talk.

Sometime later that night Sharyn arrived at the nurses' quarters of the Alfred Hospital, where I was waiting outside, and I asked her for a lift to my mother's home in Eltham.

She obviously felt sorry for me and, even though she had no idea how to get to Eltham, she drove me to Mum's. Apparently, I found out later, I scratched her new car with my crutches too. I asked her to stay the night as it was very late and she had no idea how to get back to the city. She slept with her clothes and leather coat on, on top of the blankets on my bed. I probably passed out as I was very drunk.

The next morning we went into the kitchen and met my mum. I'm not sure who got the bigger shock, as my mum was doing what was quite normal for her, sitting at her laminex kitchen table having a cigarette and drinking beer in the early hours of the morning. (Sharyn came from a family of non-drinkers.) Mum made it very clear that she thought I'd brought home some floozy. It wasn't a good start to the relationship.

Despite our 13-year age difference, Sharyn and I became very close and within a few weeks we were hooked, seeing each other every day. Sharyn still has a card I gave her two weeks after we started together saying, "I love you".

This new situation was not without difficulty. As far as Sharyn's parents were concerned she was living in the nurses' quarters at the Alfred Hospital. She was only 18 years old and the apple of her dad's eye. Her poor dad was not happy about our relationship. He was a proud and powerful man in the world of horse and greyhound racing and if he had ever found out I was abusive towards Sharyn, he would have had a contract put out on me. Sharyn's dad Bernie and I would, in the end, become very good mates and I loved him dearly; unfortunately, he died far too young and did not see our kids grow up.

For a few months we slept most nights in my bedroom at Mum's house, as when I left Ann and our rental home in Brighton I also left almost all my possessions including my car, so it was a matter of starting over.

I'm sure it was the best thing to do at the time. It would have been a bitter fight over the furniture and other material possessions that Ann and I had accumulated.

Living at Mum's was far from ideal, as she was set in her ways and often had people in the house, drinking far too much and I was still drinking heavily.

On one occasion I remember being in the kitchen with a group of Mum's friends (I was probably drunk too), including a very large and loud woman, who was driving me nuts and was sitting in a chair that my dad had always used. When I asked her to get out of the chair she argued with me, stood up, took off one of her shoes and smashed me across the face with it.

It was definitely time for us to move and get out on our own.

I was back at work on the construction of a building known as Nauru House in Exhibition Street, Melbourne. I loved working on this site. The principal contractor was Civil and Civic, owned by the Lend Lease Corporation, and all the contractors onsite came under the Lend Lease umbrella. The work was hard and at times dangerous but the bond between a group of my workmates and me was such that we came to trust each other with our lives.

One risky work practice involved the high-rise lift cars being delivered on the back of a semi to the site in Exhibition Street. I would climb onto the roof of the passenger lift car. The dogman, communicating with the crane driver, would hitch the chains of the Favco tower crane positioned above the fifty-second floor of the building. I would stay on the roof of the lift car, holding onto the lifting chains. The operation involved raising the load above the fifty-second floor, positioning the guide rollers on the top and bottom of the lift car onto the guide rails in the lift shaft and then riding the lift car down the lift shaft. Then I would ride the lift car all the way down to the basement.

This dangerous practice of riding a crane load has been banned for many years in compliance with the Occupational Health and Safety Act. At the time, it was just what we did. I'm not saying it was clever, but we really did trust each other with our lives.

Chapter 12:
Working (and living) hard

When we moved out of Mum's, Sharyn and I rented a tiny room in a hotel at the rear of the Nauru House construction site, known as Annabelles, in Alfred Place. This was to be our home for the next three months. It wasn't the best environment for me, with a drinking problem, to be living in a hotel. We also both smoked lots of marijuana daily. It was a very different world as unbeknownst to us it had community bathrooms and a very different clientele. Although we kept to ourselves, of a weekend the upstairs ballroom held functions of all descriptions. It wasn't unusual to see people going up and down from the ballroom in all sorts of costumes, ranging from animals and transvestites to some of the most bizarre sights we'd ever seen.

Our room also became a place that our so-called friends and workmates would come to at lunchtime, usually to smoke a joint, and then again after work and any time that suited them to drink and smoke weed and hang out and play music and talk all sorts of bullshit.

It wasn't long until we became absorbed in this seedy lifestyle, going out at night to meet with people and buy drugs. It doesn't take long when associating with this activity and the people it attracts to bring yourself and all around you down to a level that deep down you know is not good and can only lead to disaster.

Today, as I write this book, there is nothing more clear to me – if you associate with turkeys you'll become one. To soar like an eagle you need to surround yourself with positive, motivated, successful people. There has never been a truer saying than "Surround yourself with those who lift you UP, not drag you down!"

Fortunately, Sharyn and I had good jobs and could function at what we thought was a normal existence. After about three months we left Annabelle's and rented a flat in Tivoli Road, South Yarra. It was a perfect location, close to our work, and quite a few nurses lived in the same block. Some were country girls and they became friends and we had lots of fun.

We lived in Tivoli Road for 12 months and were both working hard. By this time I was accepted by Sharyn's parents as, if not the ideal partner, at least one that was sticking around. I was still drinking too much and refused to see that I had the slightest problem.

One night I was very drunk at a function for Sharyn's grandmother's birthday and became violent towards Sharyn when we got home. (I had no memory of this so obviously I did have a huge drinking problem.) The next day Sharyn and her friend moved out and took almost everything from the flat. Most of it was hers anyway.

I bought a second-hand mattress and stayed in the flat for a while, probably drinking even more. During this time in our flat in South Yarra, I was having an affair with a barmaid in a local watering hole. Once again, I was stuffing up my life.

Sharyn moved into a unit in Toorak Road on her own. Eventually we reconnected and I moved back in, determined to make our relationship work.

Although once again our place became a convenient hangout for my so-called friends to call in and bomb out after drinking and smoking dope. Sometimes it was a fun place to be and we both continued to hold down good jobs. There were also down sides, as there always are with this type of lifestyle.

One beautiful young man would often sit on the end of our bed and play his guitar and sing to us. He was the image of a very young Rod Stewart, had a beautiful voice and played guitar very well. He travelled to Nepal with another friend and while in Kathmandu dealing drugs he had some heroin, overdosed and died – a terrible waste of a life for a young man and close friend.

I was in total denial about my own health, thinking instead that I was invincible. Every morning without fail I would vomit into the toilet, then shortly after need a beer to function, and that would set the scene for the next day.

I don't know how or why Sharyn put up with me.

Somehow I was still able to work hard in the manic environment of high-rise construction in Melbourne. The tension onsite between the Builders Labourers Federation, the dominant and powerful industrial trade union at the time, and the major construction companies was often out of control.

Some of the sites I worked on included the 60-storey tower at Collins Place, the State Bank Building, Ansett House and the Stock Exchange Building at 530 Collins Street. My role as general foreman was to design and manage the installation of the high-tech, high-speed passenger lifts to ensure compliance with current regulations and Australian Standards in conjunction with state government Department of Labour inspectors.

Sharyn was still nursing at the Alfred, working with patients who were extremely unwell and dealing with situations that most of us outside the medical field could never comprehend.

After 12 months of living in Toorak Road, we decided to have a holiday and drove Sharyn's Holden Gemini to Queensland. We stayed in Tewantin, a suburb of Noosa on the Noosa River. It was a terrific holiday – boating, fishing and soaking up the sun. Sharyn had done some investigation prior to going away and discovered that I was divorced. (I was so stupid with my life that I had no idea that my wife Zandra had obtained a divorce to enable her to remarry.)

We decided to get married, although we both had doubts that it would be successful. However, we made a commitment and became engaged while in Queensland.

*Ron Senior (my Dad) after enlisting in the Army around
1940, when he was 22 years old.*

Ron Senior (on the white horse) in Egypt during WWII, circa 1941. I love this photo.

Winning a horse race in Wesburn in 1961. I wasn't popular, as the owner and trainer had backed the second horse to win.

What a cute little kid I was, around three years of age,
circa 1947.

Me with my much loved footy, which I often took to bed, circa 1952.

I thought that I was pretty cool, camping at Wilsons Promontory, 1976.

One of the lowest points in my life health wise. In 1977, aged 33, I weighed 97 kg, with a body full of baggage and beer.

Me and Sharyn at a party in our early days, 1977.

Our wedding in Sherbrooke Forest in the Dandenongs, 1979. We were both wondering, "What the hell are we doing?!"

Lakeside Marathon 1987. This was to be my personal best time for the marathon.

Coburg 24-hour Ultramarathon 1988. I was feeling good at the 60 km mark with my old mate Cliff Young.

Me, Adam and Rebekah on holiday in Torquay, 1991.

Chapter 13:
Wake-up call

Sharyn organised all of the details for the wedding. It was a small and informal ceremony at the Uniting Church in Monbulk on the 24th of March 1979 in the beautiful Dandenong Ranges, 42 kilometres east of Melbourne. Sharyn's parents, my mum and a few close family and friends made up the small group of 20 people who attended. We had photos taken amongst the beautiful ferns and abundant bush in this wonderful part of the world. The reception was held nearby at the Swagman Restaurant. Despite the happy occasion, we argued constantly because Sharyn's niece Nicole and nephew Scott attended but my daughter Megan wasn't there. I still had a very close connection with her.

We continued our life and work from our Toorak Road unit, but we still had so-called friends at our home most nights. Two months after our wedding, I became very unwell and ended up back in the Alfred with bilateral pneumonia. This was a traumatic time as initially the doctors thought I had lung cancer and I went through a battery of invasive tests. With hindsight, this was another important turning point in my life.

Towards the end of my two-week stay in the Alfred, and still feeling terrible and not at all the super man that I was kidding myself to be, a young, attractive female registrar (now a well-known oncologist on the Mornington

Peninsula) sat on the end of my bed and told me that if I continued with my current lifestyle I most likely wouldn't live until I was 40. I was 35 at the time.

This resonated in my thick head that the time had come to wake up to myself, take responsibility for my actions and stop feeling sorry for myself. I had so much in my life, but was not living to my full potential and my health was suffering. I was still feeling tremendous guilt about all that had happened in my life, and I was suppressing so many of my feelings and always trying to hide my emotions with alcohol.

I now know that all actions have consequences and lifestyle choices determine who and what we become.

Sharyn and her dad took it upon themselves to end our lease in South Yarra. They rented a house in Aspendale, a south-eastern suburb 27 kilometres from Melbourne beside Port Philip Bay and close to the train station for easy transport to the city and work. They moved all of our belongings so that when I was discharged from hospital I went directly to our new place.

The plus side was that I knew nobody in the area and stopped seeing most of the so-called friends with whom I had spent so much time, except for work colleagues.

One of the biggest regrets of my life is all the time I spent with people that have added absolutely no value to my life, drinking and talking bullshit. If I put all this time together it probably adds up to years. Now at the pointy end of my life it seems such a waste, but I understand that these events lead you to where you are today.

This was my big chance. On the first day in our new home I stopped drinking. I was a very fat 96 kilograms and extremely unfit. Walking to the letterbox was an effort. I couldn't believe what my life had become and how low I had sunk.

I replaced beer with grapefruit juice and started a serious walking program. (I totally stopped drinking for six years from this point.) For the first time in years I had a personal goal – to get fit and healthy and become a better person.

I was travelling to work by train, working hard, keeping my nose clean and enjoying our life by the sea.

Chapter 14:
Marathon man

In October 1979, the course for the Melbourne Marathon went along the Nepean Highway and through Aspendale so I positioned myself there to watch the runners go by. Sharyn's sister-in-law Glenda and her friend Kath were running in it. I was so impressed to see Glenda, who was very non-athletic, running this amazing event. I immediately made up my mind that next year I would run it.

My walking became a mix of walking and jogging and I then started trying to jog along the beach. A breakthrough happened on the 6th of November (Melbourne Cup weekend) when I completed five kilometres running without stopping. My weight had come down to 83 kilograms and I was feeling good, which reflected on my personal life, and I was happy for the first time in a very long time.

By the 30th of December 1979, my weight was down to 74 kilograms, a loss of 22 kilograms in six months. I ran in my first race, a 12-kilometre cross-country with the Peninsula Road Running Club at Red Hill on the Mornington Peninsula. It was hot and hard but I was hooked. As time went by I was running most days and on March 2nd I competed in a half marathon (21 km) between Frankston and Hastings, which took me 93 minutes. I was finally becoming fit and healthy once more.

During my running years I kept a daily journal. Like the running, it was a positive habit. Referring to it years later, it's easy to pick out milestone events.

On the 16th of March 1980, Sharyn was 13 weeks pregnant and had started to haemorrhage. She rang the doctor and he advised us to go to Moorabbin Hospital. Unfortunately, that night she lost the baby. Sharyn harboured lots of self-blame and it was an emotional time, but we believed things happened for a reason and we could try again in a month.

We got back to our lives, working hard, and I continued to run, not drink and feel good.

On the 31st of March 1980, thanks to help from Sharyn's dad Bernie, we paid a deposit on a house in Frankston. We were due to move in on July 5th and were so excited.

In the meantime, on the 15th of June I competed in my first marathon, conducted by the Victorian Marathon Club at Crib Point on the Mornington Peninsula. The course was four laps of 10 km and a 2.2 km loop to the finish.

The conditions were very cold and wet and it was tough, but I stuck to my race plan and finished the 42.2 kilometres in a time of 3h 29m. I was ecstatic and so very proud of myself and how far I'd come in such a short period. I'd set myself a goal, and achieved it, in a very good time. It was immensely rewarding, as I knew I'd let myself down so many times in the past.

This small but important success proved to me that by hard work and doing all of the little things right, with good nutrition, emotionally being in a good head space and being at peace with myself, that almost anything is possible.

On the 5th of July we moved into our new house. At last we had a real home; a small 12-square place close to

Kananook railway station. We loved it and worked hard to fix the garden. Sharyn, especially, turned this first house into our home.

Sharyn was pregnant again and we were excited but nervous after losing the baby a few months before. She stopped smoking and did everything in her power to ensure that we had a healthy pregnancy this time around.

Sunday the 12th of October, one year after watching the Melbourne Marathon go past in Aspendale, I lined up at the start of this year's race in our hometown of Frankston. My weight was now 67 kilograms – an extraordinary 29 kilograms lighter than when I was released from hospital 15 months earlier. I felt good until the 35-kilometre mark, then battled a head wind along Fitzroy Street and St Kilda Road until the finish at the Melbourne Town Hall (where my dad had signed up to fight in the war, more than 40 years ago).

I was exhausted but ecstatic that I had far exceeded my goal. I completed the marathon in 3h 20m 5s and finally believed that I'd conquered my alcohol and lifestyle addictions for good.

Chapter 15:
The struggle for life

One Monday early in January 1981, Sharyn rang me at work as things were moving along with the baby, albeit five weeks too soon. I came home and took her to Moorabbin Hospital. At 2.04am the next morning our son Adam Martin Smith came into the world.

Sharyn and Adam were doing well, but by the time they were due to come home Adam had developed jaundice and the matron told us the baby would have to stay in hospital for a few days. Sharyn was so upset at the idea of going home without him. The old matron calmly told her to go home and rest as once her baby went home her life would never be the same. How right she was. Adam remained in hospital a further 10 days and then we got to finally take our precious bundle home.

I was still busy working in the high-pressure world of high-rise construction in the Melbourne CBD, while Sharyn had resigned from the Alfred and was enjoying being a full-time mum with our little man.

My running continued and I was steadily improving. On March 14th, I competed in a 55-kilometre race from Frankston to Portsea. It was tough, and I finished in 5h 17m.

I was now mixing swimming, weights and punching a heavy bag in the gym with my running program. I was also attempting to encourage workmates and friends to think about eating well, doing some exercise and cutting back on alcohol, with not much success. Most thought that I was a freak, and boring, and many went on to develop chronic diseases. Several died far too young from their unhealthy lifestyles. I knew that not that long ago, I was just like them.

Persistent racing with the Peninsula Road Running Club was paying off. I won a 12-kilometre road race at Langwarrin in 41m 3s, winning by more than a minute, by far my best effort. With my new-found confidence, I'd become competitive in most of the club events.

On the 18th of October 1981, I ran my second Melbourne Marathon in 3h 13m 29s, a new personal best. In addition, Sharyn was pregnant again and life was good; we were both excited and happy. By the end of December, according to my diary, I'd run just over 5000 kilometres for the year.

The new year began, Adam had his first birthday, and life felt perfect. But a few short weeks later, our perfect life turned upside-down.

I was still keeping a journal of my training schedule and can now look back on the events that occurred over the next few months.

One Saturday morning in mid-January I arrived home from a run to find Sharyn bleeding and in labour. We drove to Moorabbin Hospital and met Dr Lubransky. He examined Sharyn and was concerned she was going to deliver very prematurely, and organised an ambulance to transfer us to the Mercy Hospital in Melbourne as the birth was 13 weeks too early.

A team of specialist doctors met us on arrival and our daughter, Rebekah Joy Smith, was born just minutes later at 10.15. The doctors met with us and explained that, because of the prematurity of the vital organs, it was unlikely she would survive more than a few hours. She weighed just 1100 grams.

Over the next few days, Rebekah kept hanging in, with constant attention in the intensive care ward. Sharyn's dad Bernie was a positive influence on us, as he had faith she would survive. On day six Rebekah's weight had dropped to 974 grams and we learned there was a problem with a valve in her heart. I was spending a lot of time in the hospital. Glenda, Sharyn's sister-in-law, and Sharyn's mum and dad were helping with Adam as it was a day-to-day existence.

The doctors were trying a drug called endomethazone to address the heart problem. It would take three days to know whether or not it would work. The wait was torturous and then we were told that it had failed to fix the problem.

Just 17 days into her short life, Rebekah was transferred by neonatal intensive care ambulance to the Royal Children's Hospital for heart surgery.

It was an agonising wait at the Children's Hospital. Seeing that tiny little body wheeled into the operating theatre, we wondered how the doctors could operate on something so small and fragile. Three days later, Rebekah was back at the Mercy on a respirator with one lung slightly collapsed. Then she suffered a brain haemorrhage. Our poor little girl couldn't take a trick, but she was hanging on.

On day 23, I was back at work, and visited the hospital at lunchtime. While I was looking at Rebekah I noticed that the heart monitor wasn't showing a heartbeat and she appeared to be going blue. All of a sudden there was panic. She'd stopped breathing.

Thank goodness the doctors and nurses were able to revive her. I always felt that I was meant to be there at that precise moment.

Day 31 and Rebekah was still fighting. She was wrapped in glad wrap, wearing, a little pink bonnet, and covered in alfoil in the incubator. The days were up and down and she went through infection after infection, which the doctors kept telling us would kill her. She was on an intravenous drip that had to be re-sited every few days, and when they ran out of spots to insert it she had to have it in her head, which looked terrible. She was being given antibiotics and had blood transfusions constantly. Many years later, when AIDS appeared, she had to be tested as she had had so many blood donations.

On day 40, we were allowed to nurse her for the first time. She weighed 1260 grams. A couple of days later she was moved out of intensive care into the first of four nursery stages. Her health went through so many ups and downs (as did our emotions) and by mid-April (13 weeks after her birth and on her due date) her weight was 2.7 kilograms.

Finally, on April 30th, we brought Rebekah home after this long and emotional battle. Our newspaper birth notice read:

Smith (Strong) – Sharyn, Ron and Adam welcome home their very special daughter and sister Rebekah Joy, 13 weeks premature, 2 pound 7 ounces. Special thanks to MMH intensive care and special care nursery.

We spent many years returning to the Mercy for testing and, apart from an admission to Frankston Hospital for bronchiolitis, Rebekah remained well, although she had some obvious learning difficulties.

As I write this, Rebekah is 36 years old and married with

two beautiful daughters, Ebony and Savannah. They are the absolute joy of our lives.

It's a pity that Bernie, Sharyn's dad, didn't live long enough to see Rebekah's outcome. He never gave up hope of her survival.

In the early years of our marriage, when Adam and Rebekah were young, we often had Megan for a weekend or short holiday. Rebekah's third birthday we rented a caravan at Cowes on Phillip Island. Megan stayed with us and Adam and Rebekah loved her as a big sister.

Another time Megan stayed with us, we were living in Redbourne Avenue, Mt Eliza, and we all went to a carnival in Frankston. I went on the Cha Cha with Megan, and when we got off the ride I was ill and realised I was getting old. We laughed about it afterwards.

From the very start we discussed June with Megan, and why the family situation was as it was.

It was around this time that I gave Megan a suitcase full of June's possessions – photos, clothes, jewellery, knick-knacks and so on. I'm sure it was because of this gesture that this was the last of the visits. (Alan never liked Megan having any contact with us.)

Later, during Megan's teenage years I rang her and told her about June's family. I shared details of her grandparents, June's brother and sister, cousins, where they lived and some family history. After this conversation, Alan rang late at night, very upset and angry; he sounded drunk and told me to never talk to Megan about this shit again (i.e. about Megan's family). I told him to grow up and not to talk like that to me ever again.

The relationship between me, Glenda my sister and Megan has been guarded ever since, as everyone in the family has tried to shield Alan from knowing about any meeting, relationship or Facebook contact between Megan and myself.

Alan passed away in June 2017 and so far nothing has changed. I always thought it would after Alan passed. (He had chronic health conditions for most of his life.) And my intention in my own mind has always been to support, love and do anything that I can to add value to Megan's life.

Sharyn and I went to Alan's funeral in country Victoria. It was a sad, sobering experience, as I could find no compassion or sadness for this man that I had known for 55 years. He was a groomsman for my wedding to Zandra, 54 years ago, and best man at my wedding to Sharyn.

Listening to those who spoke about his life, all that could be said was that he was a taciturn old man who went fishing and was often referred to as a "grumpy old bastard". How sad that a person can go through a lifetime without adding anything worthwhile to humanity.

My running and training continued as part of my coping mechanism, with the stress and emotion of Rebekah's birth and survival journey. Looking back, I had thrown caution to the wind with my training regime and racing. I competed in a half marathon that started in Frankston and finished in Hastings. I decided to run with the lead group that included two Australian Olympic distance athletes, Gary Henry and Dave Chettle. I pushed hard from the start, mainly to experience how fast and hard these athletes were able to run. I tired over the last few kilometres and hung on to run ninth overall, with more than a thousand people in the race, in a time of 1h 17m 17s.

I was over the moon and convinced that most of the time we put limits on what we think is possible. The saying "Just do it" is such a wonderful slogan. Three years earlier, in 1979, I competed in the same race and my time then was 1h 33m, an improvement this time of 15m 43s, which equates to 4.4 kilometres. So let's not put restrictions on what we think is possible. I was happy with the time of 93 minutes in 1979 and thought then that, at my level of running, it was probably as good as I could ever hope to achieve.

Life continued. We were having trouble feeding Rebekah, which was stressful. I had knee problems and illness caused by over-training, and it was a balancing act to ensure that all aspects of my life were in synch to let me be the best father, husband and worker I could be and keep my life in sync. It was a learning curve that would take years to master, as I've discovered I have quite an addictive personality.

Late in 1983 I had further surgery to remove a cyst from the cartilage on my right knee.

It was after this that I had my first experience in a triathlon, as these were a new event in Australia. The swim leg was in the Yarra River in Fairfield, the bike and run around the surrounding parklands.

The next event at Point Lonsdale on the Bellarine Peninsula consisted of a 1.5 km swim, 60 km bike leg and 20 km run.

In March 1984 the Australian Triathlon Championships were held at the Frankston foreshore, consisting of a 2 km swim, 80 km bike ride and 20 km run. I finished in the middle of the field and felt comfortable. It was then that I realised that by backing off the pace and remaining relaxed, the bigger distances in these events was irrelevant.

The ultramarathon runner in me was born.

Chapter 16:
Further than you think possible

I was promoted to site manager in 1985. In 1987, I headed a project team for the $16 million installation of lifts and escalators at 530 Collins Street. This was a massive construction headed by Holland-Stolte-Lewis. As site manager, I was involved in presentations to win the contract, design and planning committees and then the actual construction of this impressive project, which also involved installation, safety systems, sub-contract labour and crane hire.

In 1988 I was part of a small group of Lend Lease managers to travel to London, France and Finland to study lift installation methods in conjunction with building design and construction. This was a wonderful learning experience – to actually see how different methods were used in other countries and to put into place different working strategies within our own environment was an incredible experience.

It was a blessing that at this time in my life I'd become a marathon runner. Each afternoon, after work, I went running for an hour or so, even while we were overseas. One afternoon in an industrial town called Hyvinka, 50 kilometres north of Helsinki and close to the Russian border, I took off on my run along a snow covered road and into a pine forest. It was an eerie but wonderful experience, quiet and peaceful. Nearing the top of a hill on a small track

I heard a loud crashing sound – it was a giant elk crashing down the hill through the bush. It was a moment I'll never forget. I ran back to the hotel and told the others, who had already been drinking for a couple of hours. They couldn't understand what the fuss was about.

I had a similar experience in Paris. One evening I followed the river Seine for an hour out and back. I saw so much more by running in these countries than the normal tourists could ever experience.

Our kids were growing up and ready for school. We sold our Frankston home and brought a house in Redbourne Avenue, Mt Eliza, in October 1986.

Adam started school at Mt Eliza Primary in 1987, after being in prep at Kananook Primary, and Rebekah the following year in 1988. Life was good. Our new house was in a beautiful area and we had a pool which we all enjoyed. It was like being on holiday constantly and we loved this change of scenery and the lovely village environment in which we chose to raise our children.

I'd started drinking again, in moderation. I was able to continue my running, fitness training and work. But in my mind I knew the drinking was still a weakness in me.

In November 1987, I competed in the South Melbourne Lakeside Marathon around Albert Park Lake and the surrounding area; my time of 3h 2m 45s placed me in 51st position overall.

I was to eventually run 27 official marathons and the South Melbourne marathon time was my personal best. My injured knee continued to cause problems and, following a consultation with a doctor who suggested that I retire from running and perhaps take up lawn bowls, I decided that it was time to have a serious attempt instead at long-distance ultramarathon running. I thought that by running slower, my knee wouldn't give me the same problems.

Early one Sunday morning I ran from our home in Mt Eliza to Mum's place in Eltham at a very comfortable pace, completing the 60 kilometres easily. This gave me great confidence. I believed that all the years of training and competing in running and triathlon events had built up an enormous endurance capability. I continued with my focus on running long distances at a comfortable pace, studying the power of the mind and nutrition to best fuel my body.

Another long run began at midnight on a Saturday. I left home from Mt Eliza to run to my sister's at Launching Place in the Shire of Yarra Ranges, 54 kilometres east of Melbourne and 82 kilometres from home. During the early hours of the morning it was very quiet, with no traffic. I was at peace with the environment and myself, even though fatigued.

I was running along Dorset Road, just before reaching Croydon, and crossing a small bridge when I had an out-of-body experience. Looking across my left shoulder, I saw my skeleton jogging beside me. It was only a short amount of time that we appeared to glance at each other. I felt totally comfortable with the situation and to this day, 30 years later, I remember it as though it were yesterday. (How powerful is our untapped mind?)

I completed the run to Glenda's house, tired but feeling good. Sharyn, Adam and Rebekah were there to meet me and take me home, as usual, my wonderful support team.

I decided that I needed one more major long run before my first serious ultra-race, so once again I set off at midnight on a Saturday to run to Cowes on Phillip Island, a distance of 123 kilometres. The afternoon before I drove part of the way and planted bottles of water at various points along the road, as safety was naturally a big priority.

It was a long and lonely road along the South Gippsland Highway. Sharyn and the kids met me in the small rural town of Bass at 8am, where I had some breakfast and coffee. Then I was back on the road. Next stop was San Remo, a former fishing village and now a tourism hub. Sharyn met me on the mainland end of the bridge to Phillip Island for more food and drink, gave my legs a bit of a rub, and I changed shoes and headed off over the bridge to Cowes, 17 kilometres away.

I finished at the end of the pier in Cowes, ecstatic to be able to complete this journey on my own. I learned so much about myself in those 12 hours of lonely running. The highs and lows going on in my body and mind proved to me that we humans put limitations on what we think is possible.

I'm sure that, with the correct preparation, gaining knowledge and applying ourselves in a positive environment, we can all accomplish so much more than we think is possible.

Chapter 17:
Ultramarathon man

The 24-hour race around the Coburg Athletic Track began at noon on Saturday the 13th of February 1988. The task was to run as many laps as possible by noon on Sunday.

Race rules were that walking was allowed at any time. If an athlete left the track for any reason (toilet, massage, rest, first aid etc.) it had to be at the allotted point, and they had to resume at the same point and complete the lap.

I had a terrific support crew, which included Sharyn and the kids, our friends Kevin, Julie and David, and Jill and Rob, while Elaine and Bernie (Sharyn's parents) helped with the kids.

My race plan was to run 10 laps at my own pace, walk one lap and try to eat or drink something, then run the next 10 laps and not get caught up with the pace of the other competitors. My successful training run to Phillip Island had given me the confidence to stick to my plan.

All of my training paid off and, apart from my mind wandering during the early hours of the morning and my sore feet (the track had a bitumen surface and the bitumen had built up on my shoes), I felt strong at the end of the race, finishing third out of 40 starters.

I ended up running 196 kilometres in those 24 hours. I owe so much thanks to Sharyn and the others who helped, not only with moral support, but providing food while I was tired and grumpy during the difficult stages of the race.

Later in 1988 another run sticks in my mind, when Sharyn and I were invited to attend a conference in Thredbo, NSW, run by the Lend Lease Corporation.

It was a terrific opportunity for us to have some time together; Sharyn's mum looked after the kids. We flew from Tullamarine to Merimbula, then took a small plane to Cooma and a taxi to Thredbo, where we felt like VIPs.

The conference itself was a great mix of talks, relaxation time and team bonding. Lend Lease was very good at looking after their staff. At the time I held a management position and was a Lend Lease shareholder.

Thredbo is a ski resort in the Snowy Mountains and I remember vividly a tough but terrific training run.

Starting at Thredbo Village I ran under the chairlift, up a steep grade with lots of snow on the ground. Above the highest point of the chairlift, a walking path weaved its way to the summit of Mt Kosciusko, at 2228 metres (7310 feet) Australia's highest mountain.

On arriving at the summit I turned around and ran back. It was too cold to stop.

On that long run, I saw not another soul. As I returned, my focus was on not getting lost, as I was dressed in shorts and running gear. The weather was cold and bleak, and in hindsight perhaps it was a silly idea. Nevertheless, I arrived back at the village and into a hot tub. I'd always thought that I was invincible. Sometimes the scariest times are the best.

During these couple of years I became quite successful in the ultramarathon world. Most ultra-runners were like myself, with addictive personalities and seemingly a bit weird. It was tough fitting in the enormous amount of training to be a successful ultra-runner and working in the high-stress position as site manager for Elevators Pty Ltd on the Holland-Stolte-Lewis construction site at 530 Collins Street.

Being a worker, runner, father and husband, and looking after our lovely home all became too much. Sharyn gave me an ultimatum to give up running ultramarathons and the excessive training, or there would be long-term consequences for our family.

I think I also knew the time had come to do something less demanding of our family time, so that was the end of running ultras. I continued with normal distance marathons and triathlons until 1999, when I had further knee problems. In the 20 years since I began my running in 1979, I had run 115,000 kilometres – nearly two-and-a-half times around the world – in seven different countries.

Across all those kilometres I had no mobile phone, and no headphones, music or any stimulation except being in the present moment. And I loved it. I was probably as fit as is humanly possible. My resting pulse was around 48 beats per minute; all other medical measurables were excellent.

Twenty years later, my past obsession with endurance sport was to give me quite a health scare, but for the moment, that was a long time in the future. For today, I felt invincible.

Chapter 18:
Health, safety and goodbye

In June 1990, I left my job with Elevators Pty Ltd after obtaining a position with the Victorian state government working with the Department of Labour and Industry as an inspector under the *Occupational Health and Safety Act 1985* and the *Lifts and Cranes Act 1967*.

Under the Lifts and Cranes Act, all passenger and goods lifts, escalators, tower cranes, container cranes and so on had to be inspected and tested in compliance with the Act and relevant Australian standards before going into service. A government-appointed inspector did the work, and issued a certificate of compliance to the installation company, employers and owners of the plant.

In 1995 the legislation changed and the Occupational Health and Safety (Plant) Safety Regulations became law. This put the responsibility of compliance to the relevant regulations and standards onto the installation companies, and the requirement for a government inspector to inspect lifts or cranes prior to use was no longer mandatory.

However, under the *Equipment (Public Safety) Act 1994* an inspector appointed under section 38 (1) of the *Occupational Health and Safety Act 1985* still had the power to randomly inspect plant and equipment to ensure compliance.

During the 11 years that I worked for the Victorian government, our department changed names from the

Department of Labour, to the Occupational Health and Safety Authority, to WorkCover and finally to WorkSafe. My role covered many facets of health and safety in the workplace as well as public safety issues.

Being appointed as an inspector and undertaking intensive training, combined with my direct experience, provided me with a comprehensive knowledge of the Occupational Health and Safety Act. I carried out complex investigations into workplace accidents and incidents, and spoke to OHS committees, management and employment groups in reference to the Act.

I represented WorkCover and its predecessors as an expert on lifts, cranes and heavy forklift operations in the Magistrates' Court and Coroners Court, including for an extensive investigation report to the Coroner regarding a fatal accident of a stevedore in the Port of Melbourne.

As a WorkCover field officer I was assigned to liaise with the stakeholders of Melbourne Ports, and deal with numerous workplace safety issues with large companies such as P&O Ports, Coastal Express, Brambles, Strang and Patrick Stevedores. This involved assisting in the development of various health and safety committees in association with the Melbourne Ports Corporation, the Australian Maritime Safety Authority and the Maritime Union of Australia.

Between 1994 and 1996 I was a member of a committee for the redevelopment of East Swanson Dock. In conjunction with Patrick Stevedores' management and the contractor, I had input into the design of the traffic control system in the container terminal. This traffic system won a major award at the Occupational Health and Safety awards as part of Occupational Health and Safety week in 1996.

In April 1996, *Australian Safety News* (an industry magazine) gained permission for a journalist to accompany me to record a day in the life of a safety inspector. The five-page coverage included a number of photos.

On this day I met with management of the two main stevedoring companies that manage the waterfront of Melbourne's docks, representatives of the health and safety committees, and officials of the Maritime Union of Australia. This was a normal day in my working life. Most of the time, we all took a cooperative approach to ensure that systems of work with any new plant or changes to the workplace environment were compliant with current regulations and the Occupational Health and Safety Act.

Around this time I also acted as a mentor to new field officers and inspectors from overseas (Canada, Jakarta, Bali and Fiji) and provided technical advice to staff in the field of passenger lifts, escalators, cranes and safe forklift operation.

In 1994 I was still running, going to the gym and swimming consistently, and the kids were growing up. Adam was now 15 and Rebekah 14. Sharyn was working in pathology on the Mornington Peninsula and we had booked the holiday of a lifetime to the US, Canada and Mexico in September. In late August, on Sharyn's birthday, she and the kids picked up our tickets from the travel agent; they were so excited.

Meanwhile, Mum had been sick. Her overall health was poor, but it was probably thanks to her strong constitution that she survived as long as she did. For years she lived on nothing much except cigarettes, beer and not much sleep. She was as tough as an old boot, had very strong opinions, was extremely racist, had a dislike and intolerance of

Catholics and frequently rang talkback radio to express her opinions, which were usually very one-sided. I'm sure that if she'd looked after herself with better nutrition, less alcohol, no cigarettes and more compassion for others, she would have survived until a ripe old age.

On Tuesday the 23rd of August 1994 I received a phone call at work during lunchtime, from the Eltham Shire. A cleaning lady from the council who regularly cleaned Mum's house had found Mum on the floor, semi-conscious and in a pool of blood. I met the ambulance at the Austin Hospital at 1pm. Mum was very aggressive, severely bruised and extremely confused, and she refused to cooperate with the doctor, who was black. Finally, she was committed as a non-voluntary psychiatric patient.

My sister Glenda and her son Robbie arrived at the hospital at 6.45pm. Mum was still confused, nasty and in and out of consciousness. She seemed to know that Glenda was there. We left the hospital around 8pm and drove to Mum's house in Montmorency. There was blood on both ends of her bed and on the floor, a small cupboard in her bedroom had been knocked over, the house was a mess and stunk and it looked as though it had been ransacked. After further investigation it appeared that nothing had been taken; her purse was on the fridge with money in it. We rang her neighbours and friends and discovered the last person to see her was her neighbour, Cheryl, who saw her on Monday around 1pm. Mum had complained of a pain on her left side. She was probably severely unwell and in pain for 24 hours or more.

I returned to the hospital the next day and Mum looked awful; she was very frail and semi-conscious. I met with the doctor and was told she had pneumonia, a murmur in her heart and a sodium deficiency, causing an electrolyte imbalance. The doctor asked my feelings about taking active measures to revive her if her heart failed, or something similar, and if it would be appropriate to aggressively respond with any form of resuscitation or leave her in peace and make her comfortable. I told the doctor that I would rather that she suffered no more trauma and be made comfortable; however, I was one of three children and couldn't make that decision alone without consultation with Trevor and Glenda. The doctor told me to discuss it with my family. Trevor agreed with me and Glenda said that Mum had spoken with her about this and would not want to be a vegetable in a nursing home.

We visited Mum in hospital most days over the next week; she'd now been diagnosed with a cancer in her throat. On Tuesday the 6th of September she went home to Glenda's and on Saturday the 10th I rang Mum and told her that we were going on holiday to America with the kids the next day. She said that she was OK and for us to have a good holiday. I felt that this would be the last time that I would speak to her. Once again I had feelings of guilt and wasn't sure what to do; we'd booked this trip a long time ago and the kids were excited, so off we went with Mum's blessing.

On Thursday the 15th of September Glenda rang the hotel in Anaheim, California, and told me that Mum had passed away. We discussed the possibility of me returning home and Sharyn and the kids continuing the trip and we finally decided to continue our family holiday. (When we arrived home we had a private ceremony at the cemetery with the minister to say our goodbyes.)

We did our best to enjoy our holiday. We visited Disneyland, Universal Studios, Sea World in San Diego,

Tijuana in Mexico, New York and then Toronto to stay with Sharyn's half-sister Dorothy and her husband Richard. We hired a small van and headed off to Quebec City, stopping off at different spots along the way. One of these stops was Mt St Bruno in Montreal, one of the most stunningly beautiful places we had ever seen. The language most commonly spoken was French, and the scenery and history of this place left us spellbound.

I managed to continue running and keeping up my journal on most days. During our stay in Canada I ran the Toronto Half Marathon along with 3000 entrants; it was a great atmosphere and I was able to chat to different people along the way. I always felt the running community had a special bond, no matter where in the world we came from.

Chapter 19:
Bullies and finding yourself

In 1995, one of the incidents that stands out was my daughter Rebekah having a terrible time coping with bullying at school. It was probably one of the hardest times I've had as a dad. Rebekah's health problems at birth, along with other issues, resulted in her voice being very soft and she required years of speech therapy during her younger years.

It was in Year 9 at high school that things came to a head and we were unaware of the extent of the bullying and its consequences.

I arrived home from work one day to find Rebekah on her bedroom floor, sobbing. She'd had an incident at school, everyone was being mean to her and she could no longer cope. Bullying is a terrible problem in our society and to see our beautiful, kind daughter so distraught was agonising.

Sharyn had a meeting with Rebekah's school counsellor and then with the principal without much success. We made the decision to take Rebekah out of school and went on a family holiday to Bali. This would be the first of many trips to that wonderful island.

This trip turned out to be the best thing we'd ever done for Rebekah. Being a pretty, petite, blonde 15-year-old, she was showered with affection and attention from the friendly Balinese boys. This gave her a renewed sense of confidence and her first real relationship, with a beautiful Balinese boy named Putu, with whom we continue to have a friendship to this day.

On our return, Sharyn and Rebekah investigated different schools and eventually she was enrolled at Flinders Christian College in Tyabb, where she went on to complete her VCE successfully, gaining a place to study teaching at Monash University.

Unfortunately, as events unfolded, Rebekah deferred with only three months to go in her three-year degree and never returned to complete her studies. There were some difficult times over the next few years and this devastated Sharyn and me. We've since resolved many issues and the disappointment we felt with Rebekah's life choices at the time.

Our children can make decisions that we don't necessarily agree with. We have to learn that we have no control over them and they are free spirits to make their own choices and deal with the consequences. We can only hope we've given them some basic morals and guidelines.

Also in 1995, I began instructing a self-defence class in the Docklands Gym at the World Trade Centre in Melbourne.

I was a member of the gym and had been punching the heavy bag and speedball during my workouts when the manager asked if I would run some classes.

I'd also stepped up my swimming training and competing with the Aussie Masters Swimming Club at Jubilee Park Pool in Frankston. My swimming went to a different level, by training and competing against excellent swimmers.

This enabled me to compete in my first Pier to Pub open water race, held annually in the seaside town of Lorne. This was the first of more than 60 open water swimming races I've completed.

Over the next few years I began researching the benefits of good nutrition, regular exercise, a positive attitude and the impact it has on how we age. My own journey had taught me so much, but I read extensively as well about the science and available medical evidence. I was convinced that by focusing on being well rather than reacting to illness, we had a powerful tool for becoming the best we could be, regardless of genetics, age, past lifestyle or any other influences.

I then joined forces with a friend, Julie Davey, an author who has written and illustrated children's books on positive thinking, including a book called *A for Attitude*. Julie hired a beautiful room overlooking the sea at Mt Martha on the Mornington Peninsula and we ran a series of workshops, with a focus on wellness and maintaining a positive attitude. Our workshops were highly successful and I learned that most people are naive about the importance and influence that lifestyle choices have on our wellbeing and quality of life as we age.

I was also doing my best to assist work colleagues and friends to carry out some regular exercise, eat nutritious food, stop smoking and drink in moderation – mostly to no avail.

Chapter 20:
Who would pay for that?

At the beginning of 2000, Sharyn and I attended a meditation retreat called 'Inner Peace, Inner Power' at the Brahma Kumaris, a Buddhist retreat in Frankston.

During our weekend stay we were surrounded by peace and tranquillity in this bush hideaway. I believe I had an epiphany that my calling in life was to help people to become fit and healthy, and to be the best version of themselves, by focusing on being well rather than reacting to illness.

I announced to Sharyn that I was going to leave my well-paid position with the state government – a job that provided holiday pay, sick pay, superannuation and use of a car, computer and phone – so that I could help people become fit and healthy.

Her first reaction was, "Who the hell would pay you to do that?"

"I don't know," I replied. "But let's make it work."

We put a plan together to set up a business, and I began formal studies at night and weekends to obtain some tertiary qualifications. I've continued to pursue my passion in health and wellbeing ever since.

Our plan was to set up a specific exercise studio environment in our home to encourage clientele who did not like or would not go to conventional gyms. However, our home wasn't suitable for our plans so we made the decision to sell our house and find something more practical – something with the space we required, better street parking and outside access to our studio. This process took 12 months, which gave us time to formally set up our business, now known as The Centre for Lifelong Health and Fitness. We had advertising flyers and business cards printed and we hand-delivered 2000 flyers in our local neighbourhood. I met with several medical practices on the Mornington Peninsula and explained my plan to assist people that were older, unwell, overweight or for any other reason might be restricted from taking up some form of fitness program.

I bought some equipment and set up the studio. I also put a plan together so that on my first interview with a prospective client, I would carry out an assessment taking into account any injuries, restrictions and medications. Often a phone call to a client's doctor, physiotherapist or other related healthcare professional was also necessary. Then, in conjunction with the client, we'd set some goals, design a program and get to work.

I must admit, when I get something in my head I'm pretty bloody-minded and impatient, and I didn't really think all this through very clearly. In retrospect, I should have set up somewhere that I could sell later and make a little retirement nest egg.

In 2001, I had my first official client. Numbers grew steadily and after a couple of months I built my regular clientele to 25. My learning curve was steep, although it wasn't long before I realised that most of the time it was not the client's body that was holding them back from being fit and healthy, but the space between their ears.

However, those first couple of years I worked with so many fantastic people, who overcame enormous obstacles.

They included a young man who had been in a wheelchair all his life. Our paths crossed when he was a young bubbly teenager and I enjoyed his tenacity while learning to box with me. He became quite competent with his boxing skills, including punching a speed ball, floor-to-ceiling ball and the heavy punching bag.

He also showed an interest in lifting heavy weights on the bench press, so over a period of time we worked on a specific strengthening program and eventually he went on to compete in powerlifting competitions. He continued with his passion for health and fitness and is now a qualified personal trainer, employed by a large gym on the Mornington Peninsula, and helping and inspiring others to be the best they can be. He has never let his disability define him, driving, working and living life to the full.

Another person that comes to mind is a young woman who was living with her elderly mother; it happened that I had delivered a flyer into their letterbox. Shortly after that they knocked on our door. We went into the gym, sat down and she told me her story.

She was very unwell and on the waiting list for a kidney and pancreas transplant; her mother thought some form of exercise might help.

I'd never seen anybody so frail and sick in my life, and I wasn't sure I could help. However, I told them we'd do everything we could and that she could come along twice a week at no cost for as long as it took for an organ donor to become available. We started a very gentle exercise program and, after a lot of trial and error and proceeding very slowly, were able to see some progress. It took two years until she received that phone call. The operation was a success and I visited the Monash Medical Centre

Transplant Ward and spoke to a doctor after her surgery. He told me that she had done very well and believed that her improved health and strength had contributed to her recovery.

Another young man in his mid-twenties came to see me with his mother. He'd suffered a stroke at the age of nine at school and, as a result, his left arm and leg were paralysed. His mother had taken him to Europe for treatment as a teenager with not much success. So we set about working on mobility and strength training on both sides of the body; we also did a lot of boxing using his right hand. Fortunately, we got along very well and had a lot of laughs, as quite often our ideas for improving his muscle strength would not work out. I improvised and experimented with exercise equipment, resistance bands, ropes and whatever else we could come up with to improve his mobility. His great love was soccer and we would kick around a ball during every session, with lots of laughter and stuff-ups. After a while he began playing soccer for a team; eventually he represented Australia in a disabled soccer tournament. We're good friends to this day.

Often, personal training is merely a platform to give someone the confidence to do something that they were too scared to try previously.

A lovely old lady came to see me who had suffered polio as a young girl and had spent years in an infirmary. As a result she had severe contracture of her right foot, and hardly any movement at all. For most of her life, she'd used a walking stick to help with her confidence and mobility.

She was born in Scandinavia to a very well-to-do family, went to finishing school in France and married a wealthy Australian in Perth. We hit it off immediately and started off with very gentle exercises including carefully moving her right foot. It was probably after two or three years that the movement of the foot improved dramatically and was no longer a problem for her.

She regained her confidence and no longer needed to use her walking stick. She also continued her weekly exercises with me for 12 years, until in her mid-eighties she had to move into a nursing home. This was a sad time for me as we had become great mates and shared lots of laughs and stories about life. I'm convinced that the problem with her foot was that she was told not to move it all those years ago.

Another interesting old man (the same age as me), Wally, was brought along by one of his sons. He had five sons and one daughter. Wally had been a very successful businessman; however, he was now doing it tough. He was an inpatient in a psychiatric ward at one of our local hospitals, following a breakdown after his wife passed away.

On first sight, poor old Wally looked terrible. He was a big man who was stooped over with his arms hanging by his sides, his hands trembling, his hair looking like he'd just got out of bed. He had food around his mouth and all down his clothes and it looked as though he'd wet his pants.

I immediately felt sorry for him and wondered what the hell I could do to help him. I got his details from his son, including his vast amount of medication. His son left and Wally and I had a long conversation and agreed that he would come to see me once a week by taxi from the hospital. We built up a relationship during our gentle exercise routine, which included balance, posture, standing tall, walking and looking forward instead of down at the ground. It appeared to me that his medication was making him look and act like a zombie. He talked to me in detail and with such emotion about how he missed his wife and best friend. He also opened up about his life growing up, and how he loved playing tennis and cricket.

I then introduced balls into our routine and his whole demeanour changed. He had a smile on his face for the first time. We threw balls to each other left and right handed, and his coordination and posture changed. I bought a cricket bat and in our backyard I threw tennis balls to him and he hit them back without missing a beat.

After each session with the cricket bat, he would walk up and down the yard with good posture and a smile on his face. He left each session looking like a different man. However, when he arrived the next week he still looked like the first time I saw him. I spoke to his son and doctor about his improvement when he was with me and I'm sure they thought I was crazy and took no notice, or were just not interested in trying to help him. The last session he had with me he had what I thought was a heart attack. I rang an ambulance, which arrived quickly and assessed the situation; their diagnosis was that he was having a panic attack and they transported him to hospital.

I may be naive or just have a guilty conscience about my own dad. But I felt that if he were my dad, I would have thrown all of his medication into the rubbish bin and stayed with and supported him 24/7. I believe all that was wrong with him was a broken heart.

These were just a few of my special clients in those first years, when I realised that being a fitness instructor, personal trainer and someone to talk to, was not all about exercise, nutrition and working with fit, motivated people.

To this day, my work is a job I respect and a responsibility that I don't take lightly. To have the privilege to assist people with life's journey is a special gift.

In 2002, I had a fifth operation on my right knee; this time it was a total knee replacement. It was a tough time mentally and physically and the surgeon suggested that I'd need three months to recover before I resumed work. I spent 10 days in hospital and four days later was working with my leg in a brace. Over the next few years I had surgery on my nose twice and a hernia operation and I was able to continue running my business during these times. It makes me so angry when people think they can't exercise because they have an injury or something wrong.

Many parts of the body can be exercised, in many different ways, and you can always benefit from the feel-good hormones that come with a workout.

Chapter 21:
Boxing still in my blood

At the time of writing this chapter it's August 2017 and we're on holiday in New York to meet our son Adam and celebrate Sharyn's sixtieth birthday. We have a studio apartment on the corner of West End Ave and 63rd Street on the Upper West Side of Manhattan and I feel like a professional writer.

It seems like another lifetime ago that Sharyn, as an 18-year-old trainee nurse, admitted me into Ward 23 at the Alfred Hospital.

While in New York we visited Gleason's Gym in Brooklyn. Sharyn and I met a number of the trainers, all characters with big personalities – in particular Hector Roca, who has trained many champion boxers and been involved in making six movies, including Million Dollar Baby and Cinderella Man, which starred Russell Crowe, the New Zealand actor (some would say Australian). Crowe trained at Gleason's, and they shot some of the film there. Not only this film, but 25 other movies and countless TV commercials have been shot at the famous Gleason's Gym.

Gleason's is an extraordinary place, the oldest active boxing gym in the US. It's produced an incredible 134 world champs, two Olympic gold medallists and hundreds of amateur champions.

The first world champion out of Gleason's, and one of the most famous, was Jake "The Raging Bull" La Motta.

Up there with him is Muhammad Ali, then known as Cassius Clay, who trained in Gleason's Gym to fight Sonny Liston (on 25 February 1964 in Miami, Florida) for the heavyweight world championship. Clay was just 22 years old, and a massive underdog, but the unpopular Liston failed to answer the bell for the seventh round and Clay won in a technical knockout. Roberto Duran, the Panamanian superman, won three world titles while using Gleason's as a training base. (In a career spanning more than three decades, Duran would win world titles in four weight divisions.)

While Sharyn and I were visiting, I noticed a poster on the wall that resonated with me.

A Boxing Gym

In a lot of ways it is a microcosm of society, a gritty, tough, melting pot, characterised by openness and acceptance, inhabited with a lot of people with big dreams.

Our experience was very similar to my visit to Wild Card Boxing Gym in Los Angeles two years earlier, where I met with the owner, Freddie Roach. I was fortunate that, after I told him I was a small time boxing trainer from Australia, we spent a couple of hours together. He introduced me to his staff, and we discussed our journeys through life and his health issues, our philosophies on boxing, our work ethic and so on. He also introduced me to an Aussie guy training with him who had had 16 fights in the US up to that stage and was doing OK. We talked about the strict policy that Freddie Roach enforces with any boxer he takes on as a competitive professional, which is absolutely no booze, no crime and no drugs.

Freddie Roach is arguably the most noteworthy trainer in boxing today, having trained 36 world champions including Oscar de la Hoya, Manny Pacquiao and Miguel Cotto. He was inducted into the World Boxing Hall of Fame in 2008 and was the Boxing Writers Association of America Trainer of the Year in 2003, 2006, 2008, 2009 and 2010.

The feeling I get when I visit boxing gyms at this level takes me back to my own boxing days. No matter if it was in Sydney or Melbourne, the camaraderie, hard work and respect between everyone was something that money couldn't buy. Quite often the smell of sweat, the small amount of equipment, the bond between everyone training, no matter what level of boxing skill or fitness, the energy and passion in the room, raised us all to a higher level.

It still raises the hairs on the back of my neck and I love it.

Chapter 22:
Building a boxing centre

By 2004, we'd begun running boxing classes, mostly for school kids, and one-on-one boxing for adults, which became quite popular. I'd installed some heavy punching bags and speed balls. I soon realised that I was in a very fortunate position because of my boxing background and the popularity of boxing for fitness. I had a huge advantage over other personal trainers. It wasn't long before I was conducting classes for personal trainers and fitness instructors, teaching correct boxing technique, focus-pad holding, footwork and boxing combinations. All of this led to a demand to run more boxing classes, but we were restricted by lack of space in our studio gym.

We decided to investigate the possibility of buying or leasing external premises and inspected some factories and shopfronts with the help of a commercial real estate agent. However, it was difficult to find premises that were suitable for both a boxing gym and a boutique personal training studio. Local council requirements for operational and parking permits were a nightmare to work through. The problems with red tape and the frustration of not finding suitable premises helped us make up our minds to build a boxing gym in our backyard.

We weren't to know that problems with neighbours and the council restricting our operational hours meant that this was probably not the best decision.

We had a purpose-built shed nine metres long and six metres wide installed, with a boxing ring, punching bags, floor-to-ceiling bags, and a skipping and exercise section. We purchased boxing gloves, focus pads and other boxing-based exercise equipment.

Overall, this has worked out well over the years, although I'd love to have more space. We registered the shed and ring as a separate business, and named it Mt Eliza Boxing Centre.

In the years since, we've had thousands of schoolkids and adults through the Boxing Centre. I currently run 12 group boxing sessions and about 20 one-on-one boxing sessions per week, and clients range in age between six and 65.

We've had all shapes, sizes and abilities, and a vast range of personalities, with occupations that cover the full spectrum: actors, singers, tradespeople, teachers, doctors, nurses, personal trainers, exercise scientists, private investigators; the list goes on.

As with my personal training clients, I've met quite a few clients that needed extra help. I've been able to help some to work through several issues, including some teenage boys with drug addiction problems. I didn't realise the enormity of the problem in our community until I'd won the respect of some of the boys involved and they confided in me. Even young men who have finally beaten this dreaded curse after years and untold health consequences have spoken about problems with family and relationship breakdowns, financial problems that have led to crime, low self-esteem and 'where to go from here' problems. I've had limited success with some teenagers and not any luck with others. However, I believe that if Sharyn and I can listen to and provide support for these young people it's all worthwhile.

The number of young kids who have sat in our family room and talked openly and honestly about their lives to Sharyn and me is truly humbling, and something we're honoured to do. The young kids in our community know that our door is open and they're welcome to come and talk at any time.

I've also worked with a number of teenage girls one on one, and quite often we're initially contacted by the parents of teenagers, concerned with different behavioural problems like anxiety, bullying and low self-esteem. I've had some good results with the girls who have persevered with self-defence training. Once they've mastered the art of kicking, punching, elbowing and self-defence it seems to carry through to improving their self-respect and self-esteem. Often they become happier at school, at work and for life in general.

I don't know how this works, but often it does.

I've also worked with some sensitive and fragile women who have suffered trauma and contacted me to learn self-defence through boxing. I had a phone call from a 30-year-old, who told me that she was suffering from anxiety and was very nervous about returning to her workplace. She and her husband owned a business and one evening she was alone in the showroom when a man came into the premises armed with a knife and robbed her. Over time, as we worked on building her self-defence skills, she confided in me about her feelings and concerns with the business.

Her boxing and self-defence skills improved. She was becoming far more relaxed working out with me and becoming happier in herself, but she still didn't want to go back to the showroom and she and her husband decided to sell their business.

Another situation concerned a father who brought his 18-

year-old daughter along with him. She was slim and shy, and had suffered a serious ordeal at her workplace. She was studying Year 12 at school and working part time of a night. One night she and another teenage girl were cleaning up at the end of their shift when a man with a balaclava and holding a gun robbed the premises and locked the girls in a room.

She started working out with me, learning some punching and kicking techniques at a very low level. We focused on coping and defensive strategies in the early stages of our working relationship, building into more offensive self-defence situations as time went on. This has been a real success story for me as this amazing, young, successful woman now continues to box in our group sessions three years after her ordeal. With new-found confidence and passion, she's a shining light at our gym. I love my job.

One of the most rewarding experiences I've had has been our schoolkids' group boxing classes. My overriding goal has always been to help develop successful young people and not champion boxers. We've been able to teach kids the importance of teamwork in learning the skills related to boxing and life, as I believe the principles are very similar. We've adopted a system whereby the more experienced kids help with the less experienced and those who may be having some difficulty learning. I've found that the kids that take responsibility to help others eventually not only improve their own skills, but go on to become leaders at school and in their part-time jobs. I'm lucky that many who began with us as kids have kept in touch as they have grown into adults, and we're often invited to different milestones in their lives, as they grow up, find partners and start families.

Chapter 23:
Health scare

When I quit extreme long-distance events for family reasons, I was probably the fittest I'd ever been. And 20 years after that period of my life, I was still exceptionally fit and healthy. Which is why I was gutted to be diagnosed with atrial fibrillation (AF).

AF is a common type of heart rhythm disorder (arrhythmia) characterised by a rapid and irregular heartbeat. If you have AF, the electrical signals that control your heartbeat are abnormal.

Following extensive examination and testing with a cardiac specialist at Epworth Hospital in Melbourne, I was given the all clear to continue exercising, as I still do to this day. (I'd had a total knee replacement before this and was no longer able to run.) During this period the episodes of my heart racing were frequent and disturbing. To help, I set myself up with a small meditation area behind the new boxing gym. After some time and lots of practice I found that I could not only calm my stressful mind but also slow down my heartbeat.

I've researched AF and discovered that a correlation between endurance athletes and AF is common. A recent study, 'Atrial fibrillation in athletes: Pathophysiology, clinical presentation, evaluation and management', concluded:

Atrial fibrillation (AF) is the most common cardiac arrhythmia in athletes, especially in middle-aged athletes. Studies have demonstrated that athletes who engage in endurance sports such as runners, cyclists and skiers are more prone to AF than other athletes.

*Mohit Turagam, Greg Flaker, Poonam Velagapudi &
Martin Alpert,* Journal of Atrial Fibrillation *(2016)*

However, the general consensus from the studies I've investigated is that physical inactivity and a sedentary lifestyle are a far bigger health problem for most people than excessive activity.

The AF study also found that more leisurely activities such as brisk walking or cycling at age 60, even if more than 60 minutes a day, were associated with a 13% decrease in AF compared with those who got no exercise at all.

An accompanying editorial suggested that when it comes to exercising, "maximum cardiovascular benefits are obtained if performed at moderate doses, while these positive aspects are lost with (very high) intensity and prolonged efforts" (*Journal of Atrial Fibrillation*).

Other possible causes of AF include intense stress and anger, and I believe this was the trigger for my first AF episode. It was around this time one of our neighbours began to complain about our new business. This affected me to the extent that, mentally and physically, I was wound up for days on end, focusing on how I could cope with this person who was so unhappy about our operations.

This issue is still underlying in my mind, but I tell myself most days that it's not what happens to us, but how we react to it.

Chapter 24:
A family reunited

In June 2004, Sharyn and I arrived home after a weekend in Hobart to celebrate my sixtieth birthday with our son Adam. I answered a telephone call. I can still remember that it rang on our bedroom phone and I lay on the bed and said hello. A female voice answered and asked if I was Ronald Martin Smith. I said yes and she asked if I had three daughters, Sheree, Kelly and Deborah. I answered yes again and she told me that she was my daughter, Kelly.

I went quiet, speechless, shocked, as I had not had any contact with my girls for 30 years, apart from a few letters from Debbie years before.

Once we'd settled down we talked for ages and Kelly told me that she was married to Steven and had three children, Christopher, Jamie and Chloe. Sheree (my eldest) had been married and was now divorced and had two boys, Ryan and Tyler, while Debbie (the youngest) was married to David, with three girls, Hayley, Emma and Leah. Kelly gave me her phone number and agreed that we needed to catch-up in person soon.

I lost the plot after the phone call, feeling guilt and excitement mixed with happiness and sadness all at once. I sobbed and trembled and, fortunately, Sharyn was with me for support as she always is when the going is tough.

A few weeks after the phone call the three girls came to our home. Sheree drove down from NSW, Kelly from

Greensborough and Debbie from Langwarrin. It was a surreal and emotional moment, as the last time I saw them they were small children and now they were all mature adults. And it was an amazing reunion. I expected them to hate me, but we got along really well. Each of them gave me a medal that their grandmother had given them many years ago, that they had kept until now. The medals were awarded to me for winning three Victorian amateur boxing championships in 1960, 1961 and 1962. We talked about their lives, kids, husbands, work and also their mother Zandra, my ex-wife, and her husband Bruce.

I remember Debbie looking at our personal training studio, with all the positive sayings around the walls, and breaking down and crying, saying that now she knew where she gets all this from. She had never understood it before as most of her life was about survival, with few positive experiences.

Later, at a family function at Debbie's home in Langwarrin, Sharyn and I were very nervous about meeting Zandra and Bruce. But it worked out fine. Since then we've met on many occasions at family birthdays with everyone being respectful and polite and getting along well.

The first few years after our reunion my relationship with the girls was a bit hot and cold. I totally understand that it wasn't easy, with all the family dynamics involved. I will go to my grave still with guilt and regret for my pathetic decision to leave these three girls as I did.

However, as I'm writing this in 2017, and 13 years after that telephone call, I feel that I have a very special relationship with Sheree, Kelly and Debbie and love them all dearly.

I see more of Debbie as we live close by, with Kelly living in Greensborough and Sheree in Byron Bay, NSW.

Debbie's middle daughter Emma is 17 years old and a terrific member of our schoolkids' boxing. She's a bubbly, happy young lady and I'm so proud to show her off as my granddaughter.

So, now I feel like I'm complete, with my six children from three different mothers and 12 grandchildren.

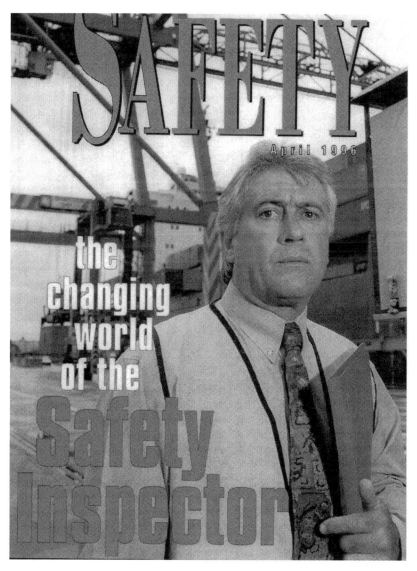

*Cover of Safety magazine, April 1996 – a day in the life of
a safety inspector.*

Riding an elephant at Chitwan National Park, Nepal, 2009.

Running a sunrise boxing session at our highest point in Nepal, 2009. Such an unforgettable moment.

Me and five of my six kids celebrating my 70th birthday in 2014.

Me and Sharyn after Rya's first eye operation in Bali,
2013. My all-time favourite nurse.

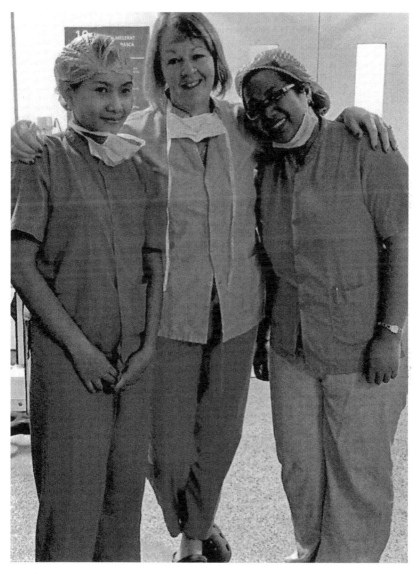

Nursing superstars in Bali, 2014, after Rya's third operation.

Me and my mate John Famechon at my 70th birthday in 2014.

Me at 71 years of age in the Bahamas, 2015. Full of life and happiness.

At my favourite swimming place, Moondah Beach, at the end of our street, 2017. How lucky am I?
(Photo courtesy Yanni.)

Presenting at our Health and Wellbeing Workshop at Lifelong Health and Fitness, 2017.

At the John Lennon memorial Strawberry Fields in Central Park, NYC, 2017.

Me and Sharyn at our headquarters, The Centre for
Lifelong Health and Fitness. Partners in crime.

Chapter 25:
Renewing vows

The year 2004 was special to us (along with our extended family) for another reason – it was our twenty-fifth wedding anniversary and we decided to renew our vows with a ceremony in Bali. On our previous three visits to Bali we'd made a special connection with some of the local people and places. We weren't to know at the time how special and connected we would become over a long period.

Our wedding vow renewal ceremony was fantastic. Sharyn organised the ceremony through Bali Jepun Wedding and the manager, Dyan Ervandi, would become a dear and close friend and like another daughter to us. The ceremony was conducted by a Hindu priest and our witnesses were our Balinese friend Putu and his German girlfriend Veronika. It was held in the beautiful gardens of a hotel in Seminyak backing onto the ocean. Afterwards, we had dinner with Putu and Veronika under a full moon.

The service and the occasion with the Hindu priest was a moment I'll never forget. Sharyn and I felt complete, unlike our original wedding where we both had doubts that it would survive. We made a new commitment to one another.

Our relationship with Bali continued after our wedding vow renewal and we would visit most years. We were lucky to find a resort that we fell in love with on our first visit as it was just by chance that Sharyn booked the Grand

Mirage Resort in Tanjung Benoa. We've since been staying at and using the Grand Mirage as our base during our travels to this magnificent island for more than 20 years. We've become good friends with many of the staff and management of the resort and as a result we're always very spoilt on our visits.

Prior to a trip in March 2012, I had become good friends with a young Balinese man called Made Arta. He and I enjoyed each other's company as we had a lot in common. He is very fit, and instructs the water aerobics, water and beach volleyball and yoga classes, plays tennis with the guests and manages the gym at the Grand Mirage Resort. The resort has upwards of 500 staff. Made is totally self-taught and has learned all of his skills from the internet. At the moment he is the manager of the water sports section of the resort, which includes sailing catamarans, taking kayak tours and managing staff. In his spare time he plays soccer for a local team.

Made is blind in one eye and has been since birth. He's an absolute professional with his attitude to work, has a terrific sense of humour and has taught himself many foreign languages – including Japanese, German, French, Russian and English – to enable him to communicate with a large variety of foreign guests. His dream has been for many years to come to Australia and work with me; however, life has dealt him a tough hand.

His daughter Rya was born with a condition called coloboma, where normal tissue in or around the eye is missing from birth. In Rya's case she has no eyelids, so both her eyes can never close, which leads to dry eyes and severe scarring. Made was born with the same condition in one eye and this is the reason for his blindness.

In 2011, his wife – Rya's mother Iriani, just 26 years of age – passed away. She was a fit young woman who taught dancing and died in Made's arms. It's unclear how she died but it was suspected to have been a massive heart attack. Apart from Made, none of the extended family speaks much English. In these small Balinese villages, where people are very poor in a financial sense, their very powerful faith in the Hindu religion seems to allow them to cope with any situation and gives them a richness to life that we (in the West) often never experience.

Sharyn and I have visited Made's village and family home on many occasions. It's a small compound, and houses all of the extended family. In this tiny area we cannot comprehend how so many people can live in such harmony, in such heat, with torrential rain, dogs, rats, chickens and small children. There is a small well with water that must be boiled and even then I don't think it's fit for human consumption. There's a small common area for cooking, and even after lots of visits I can't work out the toilet situation. The feeling I get in this family home is that it has been a refuge for generations, and the temple inside this tiny compound is an energy source that receives offerings and prayers several times during the day and night with a faith that I cannot begin to comprehend.

It was ironic that on our first visit to Bali, in 1997, Sharyn met Nyoman. She was selling T-shirts, sarongs, dresses, shorts and almost anything could be brought from her small, makeshift shop under the shade of trees on the perimeter of the Grand Mirage Resort. Along with a group of her friends, Nyoman provided massages on benches under the same shady trees. Sharyn and I would have massages on most days from these women. They were all so sweet and we would often spend time talking and listening to stories of their lives and families, with their minimal English. We still enjoy their company all these years later and always make a point of taking over a suitcase full of clothes and gifts for them and their families.

The relationship between Nyoman and Sharyn was special from the start. Nyoman is a unique and remarkable lady, around the same age as Sharyn (the Balinese don't keep records of age as we do – it's not important to them). She's also a big lady, with a lovely smile and an infectious laugh. Our goodbyes were always sad as she would cuddle us both with such honesty and sensitivity, and an immense closeness that neither of us felt with our own dysfunctional and complicated family situations.

It wasn't until a few years later, when Nyoman was telling Sharyn about her granddaughter having serious eye problems, that we realised that Nyoman was Made Arta's mother and Rya's grandmother. Sharyn and I met with Made Arta and discussed the possibility of taking him and Rya to Australia to have her eyes assessed. He told us that another friend of his was already working towards taking them to Perth to visit an eye specialist. We hoped that it would go ahead and Rya could be examined, with the possibility of surgery to improve her eyes.

Made Arta rang us later at our home in Melbourne. He was vastly disappointed, as when he had a doctor's examination as part of his application for a visa to visit Australia, he was diagnosed with TB, and was ineligible to be granted a visa.

As luck would have it during this period I was training a client, David, who worked in the field of eye surgery. He's not a doctor, but his field of expertise was to train eye surgeons in the latest eye surgery technology all around the world.

I told David about the situation in Bali regarding Rya and her dad; he was enthusiastic about the possibility of a surgeon from Perth going to Bali to assess Rya in conjunction with the John Fawcett Foundation, which is based in Sanur, Bali.

David owns an apartment in Bali and has a sense of belonging with the people the same as we do, so we felt confident in his advice.

The John Fawcett Foundation has become a big part of our lives and John Fawcett has become a trusted and hugely admired friend, whom we visit on our frequent trips to the island. John is now in his eighties and not in good health, but he's a man who, when in his presence, in his own quiet and humble way, commands respect with his words of wisdom.

John has been living in Bali since 1983, after relocating from Perth to recover from a life-threatening medical incident in 1981, which kept him hospitalised for nearly three years. He quickly recognised the great medical need on the island to treat the vast amount of cataract blind people and, with assistance from Rotary Australia and Rotary International, he began the humanitarian work which subsequently took over his life, first establishing a Cleft Lip and Palate Program in 1989 and then the Mobile Eye Clinic for Cataract Surgery in 1991. The clinic offers cataract surgery in a mobile operating theatre, free of charge for economically disadvantaged people in the villages of Bali.

There are seven million blind people in Indonesia and 4.6 million of these are cataract blind, a condition which is curable, in most cases requiring a relatively simple 30-minute operation. However, for most Indonesians the cost of a cataract operation is far beyond their financial capacity and they remain blind throughout their lives, causing a burden on their families and communities.

The John Fawcett Foundation is committed to do as much as it can to eradicate curable blindness in Indonesia and to this end is seeking funding to expand its very successful mobile eye clinic model to other economically disadvantaged areas of Indonesia.

These sophisticated mobile units take cataract surgery to the people in their villages. Experienced ophthalmic surgeons and nurses work in a sterile environment in purpose-built buses that double as operating theatres, and the postoperative results are excellent. The Bali-based clinics and teams visit other islands of Indonesia, often with the assistance of the Indonesian Air Force.

We held a fundraising event at our home to raise money to assist Rya with whatever medical intervention she needed in the future. We also had an information night about the wonderful work being carried out by the John Fawcett Foundation, at the Mornington Golf Course in their function room.

Following these events one of my personal training clients travelled to Bali and met with John Fawcett to find out first-hand how she could help the foundation. This generous woman now sponsors completely one of the mobile eye clinics operating in Bali and other economically disadvantaged areas of Indonesia.

Chapter 26:
Seeing things clearly

Following much communication between ourselves and the John Fawcett Foundation, we arranged to fly to Bali in March 2013 and meet at the Foundation with an eye specialist from Perth for an assessment of Rya's eyes. All being well, he would perform the surgery the following day.

Sharyn kept a diary of this chain of events and I'm privileged to be able to share her immediate thoughts and feelings throughout these emotional days.

Tuesday 5th March

What an amazing day. We left the Grand Mirage at 8am to pick up Made Arta, Rya, and Nyoman and travelled to the John Fawcett Foundation in Sanur. What an incredible place! Rya saw the eye specialist and we were told that she would need four operations, the first one to stabilise her left eye and do a flap then in 2–3 weeks more surgery to split the flap. We waited for hours to get the hospital paperwork organised; however we were taken to meet John Fawcett and what an inspirational man. His story is quite amazing. He is now 80 and still very involved.

So many inspiring stories were told to us by John and we met so many amazing characters. How lucky are we to be in this situation and so close to the people. I will never forget today. I'm really looking forward to tomorrow and hope that it all goes smoothly. We need to come up with ways to support John Fawcett and his incredible work. We will put our heads together when we get home. I admire him so much and we must continue to keep his work going. We all had lunch in Sanur and then drove to Celuk to the RS Ganesha Hospital, a private hospital, however very basic. I had to physically restrain Rya to have her blood test. I was so happy later when I left and she gave me a warm kiss and cuddle. There was so much emotion by everyone today. Nyoman was a mess but so grateful. She and Made Arta are staying in the hospital tonight as nursing staff do not provide any care for the patients.

Wednesday 6th March

Today was one of the hardest days of my life. Up at 4.40am, breakfast at 6am and left for the hospital at 6.20, arrived at the hospital at 7.20, met with Rya, Made Arta and Nyoman. It was so emotional for us all. Rya had an IV inserted one hour before so was very sad and scared. I have never seen such an amazing bond as between Made Arta and Rya. He is such a beautiful dad. I felt so emotional watching them —he never let her go or left her side for four hours. I felt stressed about whether we were doing the right thing for her and I could have easily packed us all up and left. The conditions at the hospital are terrible. I cannot believe basic sanitation and cleanliness are so compromised. We were supposed to be first on the list at 8am but did not go to theatre until 12 midday.

It was so hard on not only Rya but all of us with the waiting around and uncertainty. Nyoman was so emotional and worried.

Sharyn was honoured to be able to go into theatre with Rya and observe the surgery standing behind the main surgeon. David was there as well.

The surgeon was amazing and did a brilliant job, however the next surgery will be in 2–6 weeks and I don't feel at all confident in the Indonesian surgeon's ability to perform it; she assisted with this first operation and she appeared to be out of her depth with this very complex case. There appears to be no choice so I must have faith that it will all be OK.

The Perth surgeon was not going to return to Bali for the next surgery so he showed the Indonesian surgeon what needed to be done and I felt her understanding of the English language didn't allow her to really understand the incredible precision and knowledge required to complete the surgery successfully. Anaesthetics leave a lot to be desired as well, but Rya came through OK.

Sharyn monitored and cared for Rya in recovery until she had woken fully and had her breathing tube removed; there wasn't a nurse in attendance all the time while Rya recovered.

I was waiting outside the hospital while Sharyn and the doctors performed the operation. Outside the front entrance were the most manic traffic conditions I have ever seen, as it is in most Asian cities. I was standing beside the front doors when a motorbike pulled up to the main entrance with three males on the bike. On the front was the driver and at the rear was a man holding the middle person. The bike stopped close to where I was standing; the men on the front and back carefully got off, and lifted and carried the middle person through the front doors and laid him on a bench just inside. It was obvious the man was dead. Eventually, somebody from the hospital came and examined the body. I felt very uneasy witnessing all this and moved to another part of the building.

Life is so different here compared to home. This situation didn't seem to cause any disruption to the lives of the crowds of people in the vicinity, although it affected me dramatically.

Sharyn and I went back to the Grand Mirage, totally drained emotionally and physically. We were invited to the management cocktail party that night and met with Juan, the hotel manager. He is a wonderful, kind man who supported Sharyn through each surgery. It was nice to be able to thank him personally for all his support and generosity, which made our stay during this difficult time more pleasant.

Next morning, our driver drove me back to the hospital to collect Made Arta, Rya and Nyoman and we took them back to their village. That afternoon Sharyn and I also went back to the village and it was so good to see the family at home and to hear Rya's laughter; her eye looked terrible, so painful and swollen.

Sharyn bathed it and applied ointment, which needed to be done four times a day, teaching Made how to do it in the safest and cleanest way. Over the next week Sharyn cleaned and dressed Rya's eye daily. The local people were so warm and kind to us, as the whole village were aware of the traumatic time this family was going through. On Friday the 15th, nine days after the operation, we took Rya and Made Arta back to the John Fawcett Foundation for a check-up. We had a meeting with John, who also signed a copy of his book for us. This was such an honour and a privilege. The next surgery was organised for three weeks' time. Back at the resort Sharyn booked her return flights for part two of the surgery.

I should be trying to sleep before flying home tonight but can't help reflecting on this amazing journey. I feel so privileged to have been part of this and to know the bond we have with this family. I will continue to feel nervous about the next surgery; it is daunting to be coming on my own and having concerns with the ability of the Indonesian surgeon that will perform the operation. I begged the Perth surgeon to return to do this surgery and he assured me it would be fine and that I was too emotionally attached to this patient!

Rya's second operation was carried out at a hospital in Denpasar on 4 April 2013. Sharyn was there with the surgeons, but believes they were out of their depth for this extremely complex procedure; she was far from happy with the outcome. Over the next 12 months Sharyn was like a dog with a bone, sending photos, emails and phone calls to the John Fawcett Foundation expressing her concerns with Rya's eye. Eventually, we met again with John himself and showed him the photographs and expressed our concerns. He immediately took this on board and organised the surgeon from Perth to reassess Rya and perform a third operation. Sharyn was once again by Rya's side with the surgeon one year later. She believes that all concerned tried with all their skill and compassion, but the outcome is still far from satisfactory.

We've been back to Bali a few times since then and have spent a lot of time with this beautiful brave little girl, her dad and grandmother, and we love them like our own family. However, we question if we should have instigated and intervened with Rya's eyes in the first place. (We have raised enough money for Rya's ongoing care and any future surgery, which remains in trust with the John Fawcett Foundation.)

Life never ceases to amaze me. As I've been writing this very chapter on Rya and the John Fawcett Foundation, we received an email informing us that John Fawcett passed away at a hospital in Perth on the 9th of September 2017, after suffering a stroke. He was 85 years old. We were so privileged to count him as a friend. John was awarded many accolades during his amazing life, including the Rotary International Award 1999 for better understanding and friendly relations between peoples of the world; the John Curtain University Medal 2003 for his humanitarian work with the sick and poor in Bali; the Order of Australia Medal 2004 for service to the community and to international relations over many years through humanitarian projects to improve health and living standards for people in Bali; the Satyalncana Kebaktian Sosial (National Indonesian Award) 2008 for his outstanding humanitarian work in Indonesia, especially in providing free cataract surgery to the poor in Bali and Nusa Tenggara Barat; and the Bishop Hale Medal 2010, awarded to former students of Hale School, Perth, recognising unselfish devotion to duty, and exemplifying Bishop Hale's philosophy of voluntary service to and in the community.

That is a striking list, and I'm sure that even after his death more tributes to this amazing man will follow.

Rest in peace, John. You'll be missed so very much and we hope the Foundation can continue to grow and prosper with the wonderful and selfless work that you started all those years ago.

Chapter 27:
Tuesdays with a champ

In 2007, through a mutual friend, I met John Famechon. All through my boxing years, John had been one of my favourite boxers and sporting identities, along with Lionel Rose, George Bracken and Max Carlos. These were the best boxers I've ever seen, to this day. John won the world featherweight title in 1969 at a time when there was only one world champion in each weight division.

John's personal record and biography make for extraordinary reading. He was born in Paris, France, on 28 March 1945 as Jean Pierre (John Peter) Famechon. He migrated to Melbourne, Australia, in May 1950. As a young man, he won the Victorian professional featherweight title in May 1964 (this was around the time I was winning my own Victorian amateur championships) and then went on to victory as the Australian featherweight champion in September 1964. Soon after, he became British champion in November 1967, and eventually won the world title in January 1969, holding it until May 1970. He fought 67 professional bouts, winning 56.

Much later though, and outside the ring, John's life would change forever. In August 1991, he flew to Sydney for a function arranged by entrepreneur Michael O'Brian. The aim was to promote a Seven network mini-series and book on the life of Lionel Rose, who was world bantamweight boxing champion when John reigned as king of the featherweights. Both the mini-series and the book were titled *Rose Against the Odds*, the former with a John Dixon original screenplay; the book adaptation was by Melbourne journalist and author Andrew Rule.

The day after the function, John and some other identities were hosted by the organisers at a relaxing afternoon at the Warwick Farm racecourse, before planning to leave Sydney on Sunday morning.

John – or Johnny or Fammo, as he always will be known to many of his fans – decided to leave the course early and jog to a nearby motel where part of his group was staying, so he could make some phone calls and try to arrange a Saturday night flight home.

As he crossed the unfamiliar divided highway outside the racecourse, he was hit by a car in one of the far lanes, the impact projecting his body almost 20 metres. The driver was a young woman and was not at fault. Doubtless the horror she experienced was no easier to bear on learning later that the man she hit was one of Australia's most cherished sporting heroes.

John was unconscious and taken by ambulance to Liverpool Hospital, where he was put on a life-support system in the intensive care unit and the extent of his injuries slowly became apparent. There was extensive bruising and cuts, internal injuries, several fractures and a dislocated left shoulder. A tracheotomy was necessary and the full extent of his trauma was a suspected brain-stem injury.

For a short while after his first EEG, the scans showed no abnormalities, and everyone hoped he might have escaped serious brain injury.

On the 16th of September John was taken from Liverpool Hospital and flown by air ambulance to

Melbourne for care at the Salvation Army Bethesda Hospital, one of the country's best rehabilitation centres, in inner suburban Richmond.

By this time, John was off the critical list but remained in a precarious state, slipping in and out of consciousness. The brain-stem injury had exacted a price, leaving him with left-side paralysis, speech difficulty and sometimes total amnesia.

His slow, painful journey away from near death continued at Bethesda until just before Christmas and his rehabilitation lasted for many months as an inpatient at two of Melbourne's public hospitals, the Royal Talbot Centre in Kew and Hampton Rehabilitation Hospital.

When he was finally discharged he moved into his partner-at-the-time Glenys's home in Mt Eliza. This was the start of a new kind of life with Glenys, a remarkable women, who is now his wife and a 1990s incarnation of Florence Nightingale.

John's next rehabilitation phase was as a day patient in Frankston. Eventually that ran its course, completing the gamut of formal institutionalised treatment. By then he'd made some small improvements, but much remained to be done. That long trail continues today.

When John and I met in 2007 we immediately hit it off; we laughed and spoke about people that we had both known during our boxing days. I was nowhere near the same class as John as a boxer, but we were competing at the same time and were able to talk about many characters common to us both.

I soon realised that John's long-term memory was perfect. Not long after our first meeting, John arranged a friend of his to bring me a very special gift which was a signed, framed collage of John's boxing memorabilia. This still remains pride of place in our boxing gym.

I decided that I needed to do something for this fantastic bloke. Although I had never met him during his boxing years, I followed his journey from afar. I'd always respected his behaviour in and out of the ring. Whenever he was interviewed in the media he was always humble and spoke of his achievements as a team effort between himself and his wonderful trainer and manager, Ambrose Palmer. He was a credit to himself, in the not-always-perfect world of boxing.

I met again with John and his wife Glenys, and offered a weekly home visit to work with him, with the intent of improving his strength, mobility, flexibility, range of motion and reflexes. At the time of writing I've been doing this for 10 years. Sometimes John comes to our gym, but most of the time I visit his home on a Tuesday morning and it has become a very enjoyable part of my life, as both John and Glenys have become very close friends. I've committed to John that I'll continue to work on his body for as long as we can physically do so.

We've shared many special occasions, including helping Glenys take John to Bali for her daughter's wedding. This was an experience, as it makes you realise how hard it is for anybody with a disability to travel by plane and then the difficulties of travelling in a country with no thought for anyone in a wheelchair. However, we had a terrific time.

Another special event was helping Glenys take John to another wonderful boxer's funeral. Lionel Rose passed away in May 2011 and the Victorian government provided a state funeral. It was a surreal day for me, as Lionel and John were my absolute idols. My journey never ceases to amaze me. How could I have ever known that one day I would take John Famechon, in a wheelchair, to Lionel Rose's funeral?

The state funeral was at Festival Hall in Melbourne and the coffin was placed where the boxing ring was positioned all those years ago. The hall was packed with many old boxers, including me, who had special memories of competing in this iconic venue. We all placed our hands on the coffin and probably had different memories and experiences; the overpowering feeling was of enormous respect.

In 2013 the Australian National Boxing Hall of Fame formed a committee to raise $180,000 to complete and erect a 2.1-metre bronze statue of John Famechon at Ballam Park in Frankston. There have been numerous fundraising events, memorabilia sales and raffles since then, and it's been a long, drawn-out process, with hiccups along the way. Over the last few years the main driver to getting this project completed has been a terrific bloke called Gary Luscombe. I'm sure that without Gary it would all have gone into the too-hard basket. I've been honoured to be involved with the project in a small way over the last couple of years too. Frankston City Council finally had an area allocated at Ballam Park, Frankston and set up the monument by placing plaques under the statue, representing every bout that John fought during his career.

On Sunday the 21st of January 2018, I felt so proud and privileged to be with hundreds of people to witness the unveiling of John's magnificent statue. It was a momentous occasion to be with so many like-minded people from all walks of life and all parts of the globe. For Sharyn and me to share this moment, especially with John's wife Glenys, her son Darren and daughters Nicole and Cherie, was immensely special.

It was also an opportunity for me to meet Ragnar Purje. Ragnar is a martial arts expert with a PhD in cognitive neuroscience. He worked with John through 1995 and 1996 following John's accident. When Ragnar first met John, the damaged ex-boxer couldn't walk or talk, but in a short time Ragnar's alternative exercise regime started to show excellent results. After so many other medical interventions had failed, it was exciting to see the results obtained by Ragnar, with the constant support of Glenys and John's courage and determination. Six years after his accident, John walked down the aisle to marry the love of his life, Glenys.

For me to finally meet Ragnar in person was such an honour, as I'd heard all about his work. Ragnar travelled from Geelong to Frankston every Saturday in the early years after John's accident. We now had the chance to discuss his initial work, and the exercise program that I'm currently working on with John.

Once again, spending time with people who lift you up never ceases to leave me feeling empowered.

During the many hours that I've worked with John, my intention has been to ensure his quality of life remains as good as possible; it's clear that what keeps him going is the absolute love he shares with Glenys. I don't believe in any form of religion, but this beautiful woman is an angel of the first degree. Glenys's support from her son Darren, and twin daughters Nicole and Cherie, and John's strength and courage – qualities that made him champion of the world – along with his sense of humour and unwavering hope that one day he will get better, are making this beautiful family unit successful.

Chapter 28:
Personal growth

During the years between 2005 until now in 2018, Sharyn and I have been conscious of developing our own personal growth. That has often included becoming uncomfortable in attempting new things, such as new business plans, travels to India, Nepal and New Zealand and getting off the tourist paths to find our own.

We've been involved in public speaking, including a regular guest spot on local radio discussing health and wellbeing. There have been articles in local newspapers and magazines and we run regular health and wellbeing workshops. Our focus is on encouraging people to become the best version of themselves, regardless of genetics, age or past lifestyle. We discuss and encourage good nutrition, regular exercise and maintaining a positive attitude, and advise on the tools and guidance to achieve these personal changes.

In 2009, Sharyn was working as a practice nurse at a large and busy medical practice on the Mornington Peninsula. However, she was becoming more and more disillusioned with the medical system, where the majority of patients were prescribed medication to treat the symptoms of lifestyle-related conditions rather than address the root cause of the condition.

In 2010, she completed her training in Certificate III & IV in Fitness (as a gym instructor, personal trainer, adult trainer and kids instructor) and later completed a Certificate of Nutrition and Diet. She registered with Kinect Australia and now works full time in our two businesses, The Centre for Lifelong Health and Fitness and Mt Eliza Boxing Centre.

With Sharyn's vast experience of more than 40 years working in all facets of nursing, her skills are invaluable in providing specialist care and advice to our clientele.

We've continued our own journey to being the best versions of ourselves that we can be, with Sharyn pursuing her lifelong passion for health, with intensive study of nutrition, based on fresh, whole foods and eliminating all processed food.

Our personal exercise routines have become a normal part of our lives, and our day-to-day duties of working with clients in personal training sessions that include a mixture of yoga, relaxation, meditation, Pilates, balance, flexibility and strength training with a special interest in nutritional medicine, chronic disease management, obesity management and assisting clients to take control of their lifestyle-related medical conditions is as rewarding as any career could possibly be.

We also continue to thrive in the beautiful environment in which we're fortunate to live, on the Mornington Peninsula and surrounds. I swim in Port Phillip Bay every Saturday and Sunday morning all year round; even though the conditions are cold and rough in winter I believe that it's so good for my body, soul and mental wellbeing.

Chapter 29:
Remarkable India

As part of our growth strategy and adventure, we booked a trip to India in October 2006, through an Indian travel agent based in New Delhi. I was nervous about this when he emailed us to make last-minute arrangements and requested that we bring him a gift of a large bottle of whiskey. However, it worked out just fine.

I've dug out my travel diary for this trip, and would love to share some of my immediate reactions to parts of this amazing journey, which not only touched our hearts but affected our souls profoundly.

On the front page of my journal I had pasted:

INSIGHT FROM THE DALAI LAMA

Our state of mind plays a major role in our day-to-day experiences as well as our physical and mental wellbeing. If a person has a calm and stable mind, this influences his or her attitude and behaviour in relation to others. In other words, if someone remains in a peaceful and tranquil state of mind, external surroundings can cause them only a limited disturbance.

On Friday the 13th of October we left home at 4pm and met our son Adam for dinner in the city. After dinner we booked into a motel near the airport and started to feel in holiday mode.

My exercise goal during the trip was to swim whenever possible, walk each day if appropriate and complete 150 push-ups each day in the hotel room.

We stopped overnight in Singapore, awoke to a very smoggy morning and enjoyed a swim in the hotel pool, then a walk to Little India, where the temples and worshipping were very moving.

The next night at 10.00 we arrived in Delhi. We were met at the airport by the hotel transport and were overwhelmed by the mass of humanity that is India.

On Monday morning we awoke in downtown Delhi after very little sleep. Noise seems to be the norm, and loud chanting started early.

We met our driver, Nandoo, and our first day was a tour of Delhi. We thought we were prepared for India, but I doubt that anyone could be the first time they actually saw and felt the heat, smell and human mass of this country.

What an experience – smog, congestion, poverty as I had never seen or imagined.

The human survival instinct in the local population blew me away, as I watched small children living on the sides of roads in rubble and rubbish that looked like our local council tip. In the back streets and laneways, electrical cables were matted together above the street canopy. There were people without limbs and with other physical or obviously emotional issues in an environment that resembled a hive of bees or ants, in hot, oppressive conditions that we Westerners can barely imagine.

Noticing again the electrical supply and wiring system, which hung between old buildings, power poles and anything that would keep the wires above the traffic, my memory flashed back to the time I was employed as a health and safety officer with the Victorian government. In addition to the disarray, the wires and poles had become a home for monkeys, vultures, rats and all types of vermin. Mix this in with the heat, monsoonal rain and the overload situations, and I wondered how these lines didn't simply burst into flame.

Bringing my focus back to the choked, cacophonous roads, Nandoo told us that good Indian drivers have four survival skills: good eyes, good horn, good brakes, and mostly good luck!

We were taken on a rickshaw ride, which was a small carriage towed by a bike ridden by a small man. He was sweating and coughing in the thick smog amongst the mass of people going about what to them is their normal way of life. I felt guilty sitting in the rickshaw with this poor man doing all the work. I would have rather walked, but we wanted to pay him – such is life in India.

On our tour we visited Parliament House, President's House, India Gate and Jama Masjid, the third largest Muslim mosque in the world, where we felt like intruders in the prayer room. Muslims pray here five times a day. Such dedication! We attended the Gandhi Memorial Museum where the eternal flame burns. It was such a serene, beautiful and peaceful place that moves your senses.

Outside the memorial gates we met a snake charmer with cobras and took it in turns to hold a basket with a snake in it; what an experience. Emotionally, it's very hard to cope with the sights that present to you. The poor children, and the filthy street dwellers who live in these tiny shanty towns or under a tarp on the side of the road, make your heart bleed for the inequality between races.

The street dwellers are known as the "Untouchables". It is so sad to see them and often they are grossly maimed to get more sympathy while begging. We had heard of these people but when you are confronted with it, it is quite different. We also visited the Red Fort, which extends for 2.2 kilometres and is a sight to behold.

We finally met with Maneet, our travel agent; his office was a small upstairs room in the hustle and bustle of uptown Delhi. He was grateful for the whiskey, quite a character, and seemed to be a lovely man.

India is such an assault to the senses that I'd like to let my diary recount my immediate reactions to this wonderful, strange country.

Tuesday morning as I look out of the window at the rear end of the hotel I watch as another day begins in Delhi, cars, trucks, tuk tuks and taxi drivers asleep in their vehicles, as the smog lies over the trees. I know that I am privileged to be here with the knowledge that I have a safe life to go back to.

We left Delhi today and flew to Varanasi and were met by the tour guide and taken to the magnificent Hotel Ganges. We thought that the spirits were with us as an eagle flew overhead as we got out of the car at the entrance to the hotel. (We have a spiritual connection with eagles, dragonflies, pelicans and feathers.) Afternoon sightseeing to Sarnath – the birth place of Buddhism, where Buddha conducted his first teachings and our knowledgeable guide was able to explain to us the stories of Gautama Buddha, the founder of Buddhism. We visited Sarnath Temple; words cannot describe the feeling of history surrounding the stupas and archaeological remains of this special place.

Sarnath Museum is the oldest historic site and houses the Museum of Archaeological Survey of India. It houses the findings and excavations at the archaeological site of Sarnath, near Varanasi in Uttar Pradesh. We then toured the streets of Varanasi. Varanasi is perhaps as old as the Indian civilisation itself.

In Indian mythology, Varanasi or Kashi is such an important place – older even than legend, and looks twice as old as both of them put together and is one of the oldest cities in the world which has been constantly inhabited.

We were taken to a silk merchant where after a display of his goods, we brought a bed cover, pillows and a table runner. (Why would anyone buy these with two more weeks of travel through India?)

The next day at 4.15am we met our guide, a Brahmin holy man.

A Brahmin is a member of the highest caste or Vana in Hinduism, which Hindu priests are responsible for teaching and maintaining sacred knowledge. We joined the pilgrimage to the holy river Ganges. Wow, what a sight; both shock and delight all at once. Along with our guide we boarded a small boat before sunrise; we floated a candle on a lotus flower in the black filthy water of the Ganges River where thousands of people mixed with locals on the banks and in boats of all shapes and sizes and watched the sunrise over this massive river. We looked on as people bathe, swim, and wash their bodies and clothes (the only source of washing water). Cremating their loved ones is done with so much dignity and tradition on the ghats (steps) of the river. We saw dead bodies waiting to be cremated, draped in beautiful fabric. We gave a basket, flowers and a candle as offering to the Ganges and made a wish for "Peace in the world". After this we were able to put our feet in the Ganges; the water felt somewhat different, heavier and softer.

After the boat ride we were blessed by a holy man; this was so special for these people to recognise us and treat us the same as our Brahmin guide.

We then walked the narrow streets of Varanasi; it is smelly and filthy and in your face, we were constantly hassled by vendors of all description. Everything costs here, even someone to mind your shoes, as some places are holy and shoes must be removed. Security is tight as there is constant threat of terror to the Hindus; the military presence is overwhelming.

We then took a flight to Khajuraho. After a day of sightseeing we travelled 180 kilometres by car through farmland and small villages to Jhansi, one of the districts of Uttar Pradesh in Northern India.

Once again we were blown away by the human spirit and survival instinct of these wonderful people, with this mix of buffalo, dogs, goats, pigs and camels, people of all shapes and sizes riding bikes, motorbikes and rickshaws in this human river of people going about their lives, providing food and shelter for their families. Once again, I feel so lucky and humble to be in the mix of it all even for a short time.

We left our driver to experience train travel. He dropped us at Jhansi station and this was an experience in itself, as nobody seemed to know what platform our train would leave from. Along with the chooks, pigs, goats and the usual crowd of people, I was standing beside a woman dressed in a sari; I noticed that without turning a hair she was urinating on the spot; this seemed to be quite common.

We boarded what we were told was the best train in India; what a shock – the smell of urine was overpowering, the train was filthy. We watch the sunset as we hurtle along and can see small villages with people going about their business and wonder if they are happy and how they manage to survive in this harsh place. We shared the carriage and entire train trip with a married couple from Vancouver, Canada. Debbie a GP and Dennis a plastic surgeon and the travel agent had organised three minders on the train for the four of us.

It was an horrendous experience arriving at Agra railway station; more of the same, beggars and women with small children asking for money. We met with our driver and as we were trying to get into the car in these hot, dirty, dusty, crowded conditions a man with no legs dragging himself along the ground was grabbing Sharyn's ankles and begging for money. Sharyn felt so ashamed that she could not even acknowledge his existence and was hurried into the car, whereby she cried in despair. We had been warned not to have any contact with beggars as there were rings of thieves and it could become dangerous. Never had we treated another human being with such disrespect.

We booked into the luxurious Jaypee Palace Hotel; it was so opulent and beautiful and it was so hard to believe that inside the hotel grounds we were in paradise; however, once outside the security gate, it was absolute chaos.

We left the hotel at 10.00 the next morning and were driven to Agra Fort; it was constructed in the mid-1500s and we were taken to where Shah Jahan spent his final days looking over to the magnificent Taj Mahal.

Shah Jahan was the fifth Mughal Emperor and reigned from 1628 to 1658, and died in 1666. He built the Taj Mahal in the memory of his wife, Mumtaz Mahal. The Taj Mahal took 20 years to construct, employing 20,000 workers and is one of the Seven Wonders of the World.

Next morning at 6.00 we arrived at the Taj Mahal at sunrise – it was magnificent, it had an aura of peace, love and harmony about it; words cannot describe this place.

Next morning we were off again, driving into Rajasthan. It was so hot and dry and once again I am amazed by the human spirit to survive and thrive in this place, with mud huts, thatched straw roofs, plastic sheets shared with buffalo, camels, goats and wild pigs. How these people manage to raise families, farm crops, sell produce and exist from day to day with a smile on their faces and the magnificent woman wearing beautiful coloured saris is a testament to the human spirit.

The drive to Jaipur was scary and we were glad to arrive safely. Jaipur was the most modern and clean city that we have seen in India. We visited the Jantar Mantar, a collection of 19 architectural astronomical instruments, built by the Rajput King Sawai Jai Singh II and completed in 1734. It features the world's largest stone sundial.

The instruments for measuring time, predicting eclipses, tracking the location of major stars as the earth orbits around the sun, ascertaining the declinations of planets, determining the celestial altitudes and related ephemerides totally astounded us. This place was amazing as these massive instruments allow the observation of astronomical positions with the naked eye. And to think that it was built nearly 300 years ago.

The next day we were on the road again to Kimsar, 370 kilometres through the desert of Rajasthan, and the next morning we had breakfast on the roof of Kimsar Fort's Grand Ballroom, with stained glass windows that shone red and green reflections on the marble walls and floor of this grand place with the beautiful local people providing the service. It reassured me as to why we were here.

The next day was another long drive through the desert and into the mountains, once again seeing woman working in these oppressive conditions, repairing roads, collecting water, looking after small children while herding sheep, goats and buffalo.

Amongst all of these profoundly humbling and sometimes troubling experiences, probably the highlight for me was while we were stopped at a service station. A very old man was sitting on an old tractor; I think that he was blind and he could not speak or understand English. We were able to communicate as two older men do, then shake hands. This was such a special feeling.

In turn, I had a bad experience on a visit to Humayun's Tomb, another very impressive building and an excellent example of Persian architecture commissioned in 1526. It houses the tomb of Mughal Emperor Humayun in Delhi. Sharyn and I were on the roof of this building, looking at the magnificent views of the surrounding parklands and the city of New Delhi in the distance.

For some reason I was standing at the edge of the building, with my mind elsewhere. Having worked on high-rise buildings for so many years perhaps I was over-confident. I tripped and came within a whisker of going over the edge. This has bothered me ever since and I can't work out how I managed to let it happen.

A life-changing event, to experience how life might change in the blink of an eye.

We continued our journey through North India and the Great Thar Desert, visiting Jaisalmer, Jodhpur and Udaipur. The contrast between wealth and poverty and the caste system is something that to us is so unfair, but the Indian people just seem to accept it for what it is. The military presence in the area towards the Pakistan border was overwhelming; constant aircraft, large vehicles carrying soldiers and goodness knows what else, along with warships when we were near the coast. Speaking to people along our travels the general consensus of the Indians was that the government spends most of its budget on defence rather than infrastructure and health.

Along our journey we probably saw the best and worst that India had to offer. Roads totally washed away by the monsoon, road blocks that went as far as the eye could see as the Indians were using dynamite as part of road and bridge works. (Indians and dynamite appeared to be a very dangerous combination and was used a bit too frequently for our liking.)

We saw traffic accidents, herds of camels, buffalo, buses and trains overflowing with humanity and animals, people hanging from doors and bodies travelling on the roof of the trains and carrying all sorts of goods including cages filled with chickens, or bikes and building materials.

After three weeks of constant travel and 5000 kilometres with our driver, he finally drove us to Udaipur Airport, arriving at 5.30am. We weren't sure why we were being dropped off so early as the place was closed. It was scary being in the middle of nowhere, not speaking Hindi and the only people at an airport in the darkness of early morning. Finally, the little facility opened and we flew to Mumbai.

On arrival we were met by another driver, who was so small he could hardly see over the steering wheel. Once again we were surrounded by the typical hassles that we had come to understand as India. Young girls were carrying babies on their backs and begging for money amongst the traffic chaos. We booked into the Holiday Inn at Juhu Beach. Across the road, from our fifth-floor window, we saw slums as far as the eye could see. It was a heartbreaking scene to think humanity has to exist under such adverse conditions.

After a short time in Mumbai, we flew down to Goa in South India for a few days, away from the chaos of the larger cities, and enjoyed some time to rest our senses at a beach resort on the Arabian Sea.

We flew back to Mumbai for a bit more sightseeing and the next day we were headed home via Singapore.

Sharyn also kept a diary on this trip, and I'll let her words sum up our experience.

As we flew out of Bombay (Mumbai) across the slum areas I began to cry – only for the feeling that I want to make some sort of positive change, but can't or more importantly won't. We met an Aussie teacher at the airport who has been teaching in Pune for the past two years and we spoke to her about her experiences. I admire people like this, who have the guts to try an alternative lifestyle and give to others in such an unselfish way.

Our trip has almost come to an end as I sit up in bed at the Intercontinental Hotel in Singapore in such grandeur and comfort, pondering what we have seen and experienced whilst in India. I feel somewhat humbled at having had this opportunity – although at times it has been extraordinarily tough, it has probably been one of the best things that I have ever done and at times the worst. I hope I will never forget the beautiful women and children's faces that we saw and that somehow I can send them peace, love and hope.

Chapter 30:
The noble art of self-defence

Between 2007 and 2013, one Sunday a month, I was taking small groups of boys from our boxing centre to the Australian Academy of Boxing in Mordialloc, Victoria.

The founder of the Academy was Dereck Herbert. He competed in the sport of boxing in England and Australia over a period of 13 years. In 1976 he retired from competition to become a trainer, gaining wider experience over the years with stints as coach and manager of the Victorian State Boxing Team, as Australian National Coaching Executive Officer, and as a boxing judge and referee. In 1990 he founded the Australian Academy of Boxing, where Boxercise was born.

Dereck and I became close friends and soon realised that we had been competing at the same time in the 1960s and had boxed against a few of the same opponents. We shared similar philosophies regarding boxing, as far as teaching young people respect for each other, concentrating on defensive skills and enjoying the sport as we both did many years ago.

Dereck held interclub boxing competitions, drawing trainers and boxers from all over Victoria. This was a fantastic way for people of all ages to learn and compete under strict supervision, as the bouts had quite different rules to conventional amateur boxing competition. Bouts varied depending on who turned up on the day; often it would be a team event. For example, if we had three boys from our gym in one corner against three from another gym in the opposite corner, the variation in size and ability would be taken into account and rules enforced by the referee such as no excessive punching to the head by the larger boys.

Everyone competing, along with all the coaches, were very happy with this system, as we all gained experience in a controlled environment. I personally loved the format and quite often if I didn't have a boy competing, I would referee or act as a judge.

I was honoured when in 2010 and 2012 I was awarded the Leo Cole Boxing Coach of the Year Award, which was presented by the Australian Academy of Boxing, and also the Hilda Herbert Service Performance Award.

In 2013, Dereck moved his Academy to Leongatha in country Victoria and due to the distance we no longer compete in his wonderful program.

However, during these years I became disillusioned with conventional amateur boxing competitions. Perhaps I am becoming old and cynical, after taking so many boys along to so many tournaments. I'm concerned now with the amount of aggression with current boxing trainers and young boxers. In my opinion the main object of today's boxing is to try and knock the opponent out with wild punches, not giving any real thought to defence.

I'm sure the popularity of MMA and UFC has influenced the current generation of young boxers. Mixed Martial Arts (MMA) is a full contact sport that allows striking, grappling and wresting (either standing or on the floor). UFC stands for the Ultimate Fighting Championship. It's a mixed martial arts competition based in Las Vegas that encourages fighting styles from multiple disciplines but enforces very few actual rules.

I was taught that boxing was the art of self-defence, with the emphasis on not getting hit and positioning yourself to ensure that when you threw a punch, it would most likely score a point.

As a result, I encourage my students not to compete and be happy with learning the wonderful skills of being competent at this noble art. However, some young people have not been content with my philosophy and have moved on to compete with other trainers.

Perhaps I'm being over-cautious, but I've felt more and more comfortable with my beliefs as these young men have become close to me. As I teach boxing and life skills to these young people, I reach the point, of course, where I don't want to see them hurt. Over many years in the boxing world, I've seen how things can go terribly wrong. It's not all about winning or losing. I'd much prefer to train a young person to become a champion person rather than a champion boxer.

One of the success stories out of our visits to Dereck Herbert's boxing competitions and the years around that time at our boxing centre was when Tom, a terrific young man who had been learning and helping me teach our boxing classes, began some part-time work at a local restaurant in Mt Eliza. He met the chef, a young man in his twenties named Marcos. Tom told Marcos that he was learning boxing at our gym and so Marcos came along to meet me. He was a fit, strong young man; however, he'd never been taught boxing before.

Marcos was a quick learner and a good athlete and it wasn't long before he became rather proficient at the art.

He had a terrific work ethic and I enjoyed teaching and working out with him. He had a few interclub boxing competitions at the Australian Boxing Academy over a period. He was matched to have a fight at the Reggio Calabria Club but this fell through.

It was after this that Marcos opened his own boxing gym in a factory in an industrial area in Mornington. The business is called Peninsula Boxing and has become very successful, training competition boxers.

Marcos has become one of Victoria's leading trainers, at times holding the position of head coach of the Victorian Amateur Boxing Association, and head coach of the national team during international competitions. I've just also heard that he'll be assistant coach of the 2018 Commonwealth Games boxing team, on the Gold Coast in Queensland.

Chapter 31:
Superules and a super rule

Sharyn and I have always enjoyed working together as a team, sorting out the challenges and the demands of operating our two businesses, and revelling in the opportunity to help our clients and friends to make positive changes to their health, wellbeing and attitude.

In 2011, we were approached by a friend to become trainers for the Cranbourne Superules Football Club. We agreed to help out in the short term. Superules is a competition of Australian Rules Football for players over the age of 35, with games on a Sunday every fortnight. Cranbourne has two teams – over thirty-fives and over forties. We soon discovered that it was a serious competition and many of the players had been playing football for most of their lives. Sharyn was the official trainer and her nursing skills were invaluable, as at times the injuries to players were serious.

Our game day routine started about 90 minutes before the first fixture. I would massage players depending on their requirements regarding long-term injuries, tight muscles, sore backs and so on. Sharyn would strap ankles and shoulders, and provide advice regarding injuries, soreness and anything else that cropped up on the day. During the game we provided on-field support, treating injuries as they occurred. Sharyn also had to make a call on possible concussions, ensuring that any player receiving a knock to the head was checked out before returning to the field and even cleared by a doctor before playing again.

We carried out the same routine for the second game. At the end of games we would give players bags of ice to use on any part of the body that had been injured, in the hope of minimising the duration of the injury.

It wasn't long before we felt that we were an integral part of the team, working closely with the coaches, players and committee. We made many good friends that we still see to this day. After agreeing to help out for the short term we continued in the role of trainers for six years and found it to be a very rewarding experience, learning new skills and being a part of the team environment.

However, I was totally overwhelmed by the drinking culture of not only the players, but also the supporters, families and most of the people in this football world. (Perhaps it's a cross-section of society today that we don't see in the world of personal training and health.)

It was a shock to see players smoking, and the copious amounts of alcohol and junk food consumed were apparently a normal part of life for the majority of people we met over these six years. In 2015, two players from the Cranbourne team passed away. It was a gut-wrenching time for us all, as we were close to them and their families. Both were popular and lovely people; they'd been members of the football club committee and loved by all throughout the Superules competition.

One positive to come out of this was my own realisation that alcohol was still a problem for me. Even though I wasn't drinking to the same extent as most people we've come to know, it was physically and mentally doing my head in. My drinking consisted of having two beers on

Thursday, Friday, Saturday and Sunday nights. I could justify in my mind that this was OK. However, I'd noticed that my nose had started to turn purple, and I felt I looked like an old drunk. Nor was I as sharp as I would have liked on the days I didn't drink, which were Mondays, Tuesdays and Wednesdays. I felt that my head was scrambled and I was constantly hanging out for Thursdays so I could justify a drink. I thought I was doing the right thing by having a few alcohol-free days per week.

I had a routine colonoscopy which showed I had two polyps. I was shocked that my body wasn't as perfect as I thought. Polyps are pre-cancerous and there's a strong connection between cancer and alcohol.

The penny finally dropped. On Father's Day in 2015, I decided to stop drinking alcohol completely. Two-and-a-half years later, this is one of the best decisions I've ever made. I have no anxiety about not drinking and no desire to ever drink again.

On reflection, while writing about my journey, I've realised that alcohol has been involved in one way or another in most of the poor decisions I've made in life.

The Serenity Prayer, written by an American theologian in the 1930s, is a common mantra for many people, and has helped me too in making this lifetime commitment.

Grant me the serenity to accept the things I cannot change, the courage to change the things I can, and the wisdom to know the difference

Alcoholics Anonymous and other 12-step addiction programs have adopted the Serenity Prayer, in various versions, and it's often used around the world to open and close meetings.

Chapter 32:
Ups and downs in Nepal

Our spiritual and personal growth adventures continued in March 2009, when we decided to trek in Nepal. We actually wanted to add Nepal to our Indian expedition, but there was trouble in the region at the time and we were advised not to go. But the call of the mountains was strong. Nepal fascinated our spirit, and was also a place where a special friend had died. We had to go.

We did our homework and decided that the World Expeditions Annapurna–Chitwan 15-day trek was for us. To finally book the trip was incredible, as we'd thought and talked about trekking in the Himalayas for possibly 30 years. While we were away, in fact, we celebrated our thirtieth wedding anniversary, so we'd been talking about Nepal for as long as we'd been married.

As for India, Sharyn and I kept travel diaries that capture our reactions to this wild and spiritual landscape.

We left home with a stopover in Singapore and arrived at Kathmandu's Tribhuvan Airport. A mix of India and Bali, we were met by our driver and driven to the Radisson Hotel where we were introduced to the World Expedition representatives.

After booking into the hotel, we walked to Thamel Village. Sharyn loved the shops, there was the usual mix of beggars and security near the Royal Palace which was on high alert after all members of the Royal family had been assassinated.

We had dinner at the hotel – a mixture of Indian and Western and the food was fantastic.

At 6 the next morning looking out of our window the sky is cloudy and hazy with the sun trying to break through. I watched as a group of women performed a prayer ritual and collected flowers for the daily offerings. It's hard to believe that we are in this part of the world as it is so different from home.

We enjoyed a sightseeing trip with our driver and a young lady named Roanna, a doctor from Perth who is also in our trekking group.

We stopped at Bhaktapur, a very old city filled with local culture, situated in the Kathmandu Valley, 13 km from the capital city of Kathmandu. Our guide was a well-educated young man, 15 years of age and wise beyond his years. He explained about the history and culture that has existed for hundreds, if not thousands of years. When I said goodbye to our young guide, he shook hands and said that he would never forget me.

We had dinner with Roanna and were excited at the prospect of a sightseeing flight over Mount Everest at 7 the next morning, weather permitting. We were on our way at 5am with uncertainty about the weather as this would be the only morning that we would have available to make this flight.

I can't remember ever feeling so excited. We boarded a Buddha Air flight and left on an 18-seater plane, which flew along the Himalayan Range. Shortly after leaving we saw our first ice-capped mountain over

8000 metres high, then several more until Everest came into view. It was stunning and such a spectacular sight. It made us very emotional to be in this place and see this majestic sight together.

At the end of our flight we were presented with a certificate which read, "I did not climb Everest … but touched it with my heart." This summed our experience up perfectly. Back at the hotel, we met up with the trek leader and our hiking group.

Our first impressions were that it was a very different group than we had imagined, however after spending time over dinner at a Nepali restaurant we discovered that there were four doctors in our group of nine, one accountant, a mother and daughter and us.

The trek leader Romi told us that his "religion is humanity". His mother was Christian, his father Buddhist and he grew up a Hindu and had Muslim influences.

Next morning we travelled by bus to Pashupatinatu Temple on the Bagmati River. The temple is dedicated to Lord Shiva and was built in the 5th century.

Beside the river bodies were burning on the ghats and we could see other families preparing bodies for cremation and then lighting the fires in the throat.

It was very confronting to see the faces of the dead, however in a strange way we felt honoured to be a part of it.

Apparently they believe that to reach nirvana the bodies must be burnt within three hours of death and the remains placed into the Bagmati River, the most holy river in Nepal and which runs into the Ganges River in India.

Sharyn too was inspired by the landscape, and excited and a little bit apprehensive to be here, out of our comfort zone but expanding our horizons.

I have dreamed about this place for so long and it was as wonderful and filled with so much energy as I could ever have imagined. This trip has been so much more than we could ever have imagined. We hope the trek will match our expectations.

Next morning we began the day early and boarded our Yeti Air flight to Pokhara at Kathmandu Airport. A small plane with two propellers, we were all a bit nervous. However, the trip was fantastic with great views of the stunning Himalayan mountain range.

Pokhara is a city on Phewa Lake in central Nepal. It is known as a gateway to the Annapurna Circuit. World Expeditions have a permanent camp set up here as a start and finish point for various treks. We had lunch in the camp then boarded a bus for the 1-hour drive to the starting point. We got out of the bus and basically walked 2 km uphill; it was tough and exhausting and we were both shocked at how hard it was. We finally arrived at Australia Camp, where we set up our tent and sorted our gear. We were also shocked at the toilet; a small hole dug out in the ground and a commode seat over the top, which is the best that we will get, so we all got over it promptly.

There are the most magnificent views of the mountains all around. This trip will put us way out of our comfort zone but already we feel a sense of achievement at having managed this far.

The food so far has been good and the Sherpa guides are fantastic.

We felt very lucky to be celebrating our thirtieth wedding anniversary in this place.

We love this experience but feel for the beautiful Nepalese people; the poverty and political uncertainty is causing such grief.

For dinner, the cook made us an anniversary cake and Romi our trek leader gave us a card and present.

Sitting on top of a mountain on our second afternoon after a 3-hour climb we are totally exhausted. The last 2 days have become much harder, however the sights of ice-capped mountains all around us and life in what seems like the most remote place on the planet make it all worthwhile. We were so unprepared and so naive with our training regime. We still had a 2-hour walk to camp. After dinner we crawled into our tent, bunkered down and listened to a massive thunder and lightning storm and it is bitterly cold of a night.

It was a highly challenging trek. Most of the group, including me, had days and nights of feeling unwell. I'm not sure if it was because of fatigue or altitude sickness or perhaps both.

Most days consisted of going either uphill or downhill for seven or eight hours before reaching camp. We were further challenged by extreme weather, torrential rain, thunder, lightning, heat, a leaky tent, tummy aches and dreadful toilet facilities.

But challenges aside, our adventure also had the most remarkable take-your-breath-away moments, as Sharyn describes.

We are in Birethani Camp. Have felt fantastic today, although sore quads and calves. We walked 3½ hours to lunch camp this morning which was 1-hour downhill and then Nepalese flat (up and down hill) along the Modi Khola River. A really pretty area which was lush and it was nice to hear the sound of rushing water.

I'm sitting by this river and feel so lucky to be here and have this amazing experience. I love this place so much. The people are incredible, the mountain views are indescribable. I could say heavenly, serene, mystifying and godly.

The views from the top of the lodge this morning in Ghandruk were amazing. I hope the photos justify the reality.

We walked 1½ hours this afternoon to Birethani and we are camped along the banks of the Modi Khola. The food that is prepared, 3 meals a day, is amazing; the variety and quality are fantastic. There are a lot of Tibetan refugees here as well. I am feeling great although tired, but empowered and overjoyed. I can't wait to see what each new day brings. I love all our crew as we can talk and have fun along the way and their singing is beautiful.

One of the highlights of this adventure was waking at sunrise at the highest point of our trek and demonstrating some boxing techniques to the three male UK doctors who were part of our group. The team of 22 Sherpas and porters found it very interesting and amusing and before long we had a group boxing session underway, with limited English but lots of passion under an amazing sunrise on the top of the world. The power of sport with a group filled with energy and humour was such an unforgettable honour.

On arrival at Bhanjyang, the finish point of the trek, we boarded our bus to Pokhara. It was a hairy ride along narrow mountain roads. Gazing down at the sheer drops, we were disheartened to see old buses, trucks and cars that had come to grief and tumbled down the steep ravines. It seemed to be no problem for the driver or our support crew; just another day in paradise.

We arrived at the World Expeditions camp in Pokhara and a shower at last, the first since we began our incredible journey. There was a queue waiting for the shower so when it was our turn we got in together; it was ice cold, but so good to get clean.

This was our last night with our 22-man crew. After a lovely dinner, we all contributed money for the wonderful team that had kept us safe, warm and fed. We also admired these beautiful, humble Nepalese men who had put all of us first on this amazing adventure. Two of our team made speeches, while we handed out items of clothing and footwear to the porters. Ever grateful, these hardworking men are paid a pittance to carry enormous loads over the most inhospitable countryside on the planet, all the while ensuring our safety, so beautifully humble, with huge smiles and happy demeanours.

Romi, our trek leader, made a passionate, memorable speech and compared the trekking experience to life. "It was sometimes uphill and sometimes downhill but the most important thing was to put one foot in front of the other and continue on." The simple significance made me reflect on my life and once again assess how lucky I am.

The next morning we were on our way to Chitwan Jungle Lodge. The roads again were chaotic, winding through busy towns, lush rice plantations and rugged terrain.

On arrival, we transferred from our bus to a jeep and drove across a river to the Lodge. We were allocated our room with an actual single bed each, the first real bed for 13 nights, hot solar powered water in the shower, a fantastic dinner and overall we were immensely happy. We could hear lots of bird life; apparently we were surrounded by bears, tigers, elephants, rhinoceros and deer and were warned to check our belongings for scorpions.

Next morning we had a sunrise elephant safari through the jungle, where we spotted two rhinoceros, and plenty of wild boar and buffalo. Over the next two days we enjoyed jungle walks with a guide who provided information on breeding programs, the ongoing poaching problems in the country, the environmental impact of tourism and the political unrest facing this wonderful country.

We left Chitwan after a wonderful few days and we were transported by bus to Kathmandu, a six-hour, wild and bumpy trip with massive cliffs, winding roads and crazy driving. We arrived safely back to the Radisson Hotel, which was such luxury after 15 days in the mountains.

Sharyn describes the end of our trip, and sad recollections of our friend Paul, who died in Kathmandu so many years ago.

We slept in until 6.30. Romi came up to our room for a chat and cuppa. Had breakfast in the dining room with the remaining few left of the group. We walked to Thamel, which is such a haven for tourists and shoppers; it became popular during the hippie days of the '60s when many artists came to Nepal and spent many weeks based there.

We walked along Freak Street, which is a small infamous street located at the south of Kathmandu's Durbar Square. This ancient street was renamed Freak Street, which referred to the hippie trail of the 1960s and 1970s. We did lots of shopping and we were offered hashish at every corner. It seemed like the olden days and this city reminds us of Paul and we think of him losing his life in this place all those years ago.

We went back to the hotel and I had a hot bath as both feet and ankles are very swollen. We had dinner downstairs and said our goodbyes as we are off home early in the morning. I am feeling very sad to be leaving Kathmandu. I picked up a newspaper in the lobby of the hotel, which was written in English, and I was fascinated to read part of an article that resonated with me, so far from home in this unbelievable city.

A LIFE THAT MATTERS

Ready or not it will all come to an end. There will be no more sunrises, no minutes, hours or days. All the things you collected, whether treasured or forgotten will pass to someone else. Your wealth, fame and temporal power will shrivel to irrelevance. It will not matter what you owned or what you were owed.

Your grudges, resentments, frustrations and jealousies will finally disappear. So to, your hopes, ambitions, plans and to do lists will expire. The wins and losses that once seemed so important will fade away.

It won't matter where you came from or what side of the tracks you lived on in the end.

It won't matter whether you were beautiful or brilliant. Even your gender and skin colour will be irrelevant.

So what will matter?

What will matter is not what you brought but what you built, not what you got but what you gave.

What will matter is not your success but your significance.

What will matter is not what you learned but what you taught.

What will matter is every act of integrity, compassion, courage or sacrifice that enriched, empowered or encouraged others to emulate your example.

What will matter is not your competence but your character.

What will matter is not how many people you knew, but how many will feel a lasting loss when you're gone.

What will matter is not your memories but the memories that live in those who loved you.

What will matter is how long you will be remembered, by whom and for what.

Living a life that matters doesn't happen by accident.
It's not a matter of circumstance but of choice.

Choose to live a life that matters.

We flew from Kathmandu to Singapore and got a ferry to Bintan Island in Indonesia for a few days of rest and recuperation before arriving back in the 'real' world and our wonderful life, as always feeling so very grateful.

Chapter 33:
No fear

We travel to experience different cultures and meet people from all walks of life. We love getting off the tourist pathways and meeting real people. We also like to explore a place's history and significance, and when we do all this, we often form long and lasting relationships.

For all those reasons and more, in 2010 we flew from Melbourne to Christchurch, arriving at our hotel around midnight. We spent the next day exploring the city, looking forward to what New Zealand had to offer.

On Sunday morning we caught a shuttle to the Christchurch railway station; it was like going back in time, or a station out of a nursery rhyme. We boarded the TranzAlpine train, which travels 223 kilometres from Christchurch to Greymouth across the vast plains of Canterbury, passing through the magnificent Arthurs Pass National Park. The track is known as the Midland Line and is regarded as one of the world's great train journeys for the scenery through which it passes.

It was a spectacular four hours and 30 minutes of travel through snow-capped peaks, long tunnels through the mountains and beautiful countryside until we arrived in Greymouth. We hired a car, drove to Hokitika for lunch and then continued the magnificent journey through beautiful countryside until we arrived at Franz Josef Village in a small clearing in the rainforest just seven kilometres from the impressive Franz Josef Glacier.

Franz Josef Glacier is a 12-kilometre temperate maritime glacier in Westland Tai Poutini National Park on the west coast of New Zealand's South Island. Its namesake town is a magical little village, surrounded by snow-capped mountains. It was cold, wet and cloudy but it all still looked like a page out of a child's storybook.

Happy to finally arrive, we organised a helicopter flight over the Franz Josef and Fox glaciers at 10.30 the following morning, weather permitting.

The next morning, as it turned out, was overcast, wet and cold, although the views from our window were still incredible. However, the inclement weather was enough to cancel our helicopter trip.

We drove to the car park of the glacier and then walked one-and-a-half hours to the ice mass itself, a magnificent sight. The glacier provides some of the most stunning "ice architecture" of any glacier in the world. Franz Josef was still advancing in 2008, but since then has entered a rapid phase of retreat. As for most other New Zealand glaciers, which are mainly found on the eastern side of the Southern Alps, the shrinking is attributed to global warming.

Due to the collapse of the terminal face in 2012, Franz Josef proper is now only accessible by helicopter, which we hoped to experience the next day if the weather improved.

We woke the next morning to a full moon and clear skies. The helicopter flight was on and was such an amazing experience, travelling so close to the mountain face. After landing on the glacier at 2000 metres above sea level, we walked on the ice itself, soaking up this once-in-a-lifetime experience. We then continued on the sightseeing flight over Fox Glacier and towering Mt Cook (3724 m), arriving safely back in the tiny, picturesque town of Franz Josef. We did a bit more sightseeing, including a rainforest walk at night to witness glow worms lighting up the forest.

The next morning on our drive to Queenstown 400 kilometres south we witnessed the most breathtaking scenery around every corner – picture postcard stuff.

Arriving in Queenstown we met up with Sharyn's lifelong friend, Michelle.

We spent a day sightseeing, until the moment that Sharyn and Michelle had talked about since they were in their twenties arrived. They are now 53, and very tentatively they booked a skydive to take place over the Remarkables, a mountain range and ski field in Otago in the South Island. There was a palpable mixture of nerves and excitement for all three of us, although I was the support team and not jumping. Sharyn wrote about her fears, goals and ultimate sense of achievement.

I am so nervous about the jump tomorrow! Trying to psych up! Michelle seems so calm. It is going to represent "NO FEAR" for me and putting behind all of my past trials and moving forward in my life's journey. I'm currently reading The Monk Who Sold His Ferrari and a quote from the book that resonates with me is:

Build strength of character.
Develop mental toughness.
Live with courage.

These three attributes would lead to a virtuous life and a life filled with achievement, satisfaction and inner peace.

Zone of the Unknown!

The only limits on your life are those that you set yourself.

When you dare to get out of your circle of comfort and explore the unknown, you start to liberate your true potential.

This is the first step towards self-mastery and mastery over every other circumstance in your life.

I did it! ... I jumped out of what seemed to be a miniature plane from 12,000 feet above sea level. I have never felt so much fear in my life. The feeling of ascending in a plane whilst sitting on the floor tightly strapped to Greg, my jump master and lifeline, was so scary. I had totally conceded all control, which in itself is a huge thing for me.

When the door opened I felt total panic, my heart was almost beating out of my chest – the air on you was incredibly powerful ... if I had been any longer in freefall I think I would have blacked out as I was looking down and the force of air against my chest made it impossible to breathe. I was told we were freefalling at around 200 kilometres an hour. Later, I found out I should have looked at the horizon and it would have been much less dramatic. Finally the parachute opened and it was so calm, serene and peaceful floating down. The scenery was breathtakingly spectacular.

The landing was so easy and such a relief as well as so very emotional. What an incredible feeling of achievement, courage and a moment where I totally faced my fear, along with elation that there was now NOTHING that I couldn't do.

Poor Ron was so stressed watching me and was even more emotional than I was.

I know I am capable of doing whatever I want now and there is never any limit. It was so special to do it with Michelle and if it is possible to make our friendship stronger, it was in this moment. She was such a positive influence on me. I just hope it can give us the courage to be the people we deserve to be.

Our good friend Monica had also arrived and we introduced her to Michelle. The four of us adventurous souls, not knowing what to expect, then attended a 5pm trek briefing for our trip to spectacular Milford Sound.

Next morning, 38 interesting people of all ages and nationalities, along with our four female guides, climbed onto a bus in Queenstown for Te Anau, where we boarded a boat to the starting point of this world-famous trek.

It was a short hike to our lodge, Glade House, for the night, where we sorted our luggage in our allotted rooms, then went on a two-hour walk through the bush with an interesting narrative by the senior guide, Claude. We had dinner and a briefing in preparation for our 16-kilometre hike the following day.

Next morning we left Glade House to walk to our next lodge, Pompolana. It was warm and carrying a heavy backpack proved challenging. With sore knees we arrived at Pompolana exhausted, after walking through beautiful but undulating scenery. We had just got into our room when we heard a very loud crashing noise; out of the bedroom window we witnessed an avalanche, with enormous sections of snow falling from the mountain. It felt as though we were in a treehouse.

Next day we set off early and walked nine kilometres uphill; it was tough going for our little group. Sharyn, Michelle, Monica and I had our heads down and bums up, helping each other physically and mentally as at times we were waist deep in snow, forming a human chain with our walking poles. We made it across McKinnon Pass, the highest point of the trek; it was freezing, with strong, biting winds. There were magnificent views across the mountains and down to the valley, then a steep five kilometres downhill on the emergency track as the avalanche had blocked the main path. It was tough going and we were soaking wet, carrying a heavy pack and our knees were glad to finally get into camp.

We arrived at Quinton Lodge at 4.30pm and it was so good to see the sign to the accommodation, then shower and rest. Everyone was tired and sore, but spirits were high and there was lots of laughter and discussion within the group. Tomorrow would be the last walking day, 21 kilometres of fairly flat terrain, however our muscles and bodies were sore.

On our way early the next morning we found the terrain undulating and rocky. It poured with rain the entire day, which allowed us to see many beautiful waterfalls along the track, but it was extremely hard going. Wading through the water we had trouble keeping our feet stable. The mossy, slippery rocks were treacherous to walk over. Sharyn had a nasty fall just after finishing at Sand Fly

Point, which would give her some long-term grief and a severe ongoing neck injury.

What an amazing achievement for this little band of four. Presentations took place after dinner and Sharyn spoke on behalf of the group to thank our four amazing guides and all involved in making this formidable journey so informative, and expressed how these few days will remain with us for the rest of our lives.

Sharyn commented to me that perhaps we're too old and stiff in the bodies to do these long walks, especially with the track washed away and going the long way round, when we could be lying on a beach in Bali or somewhere receiving a massage. Those thoughts didn't last long, as we were always planning our next adventure. We both woke quite sore with knee problems, and Sharyn's shoulder, neck, ankles and calves were giving her grief. After breakfast we made lunch, walked down to the wharf and had a two-hour cruise through Milford Sound. The weather was warm and sunny on the way out, then cloudy and cool on the way back. It was such picturesque scenery and thoroughly enjoyable.

Our vessel took us out to the Tasman Sea; the magnificent beauty of Fiordland is incredible. Fiordland is home to the stunning fiords of Milford Sound and Doubtful Sound, the beautiful lakeside towns of Te Anau and Manapouri and this area is known as the sightseeing and walking capital of the world. We boarded the bus back to Te Anau then onto Queenstown, a very scenic journey past mountains and through tunnels. Everywhere on this South Island is so stunningly beautiful.

On arriving home in Australia we received an email from Michelle, in response to a thank you card Sharyn had sent her. It sums up our trip and the special bond between these two women, which has endured across 50 years, through good and bad times.

I sat down and read your card on Saturday night. The "soggy" reference on the front made me laugh as it was so appropriate. I don't think I will ever forget that last day in the rain. We were a real troupe and the card was so appropriate. The friendship and camaraderie between the three of us got us through the miserable conditions.

The sentiments you expressed with your beautiful words mirror mine exactly.

I feel truly blessed to have you both for my friends and your generosity in allowing me to join you on your holiday was enormous just like your hearts!

I have a feeling we will share more adventures over the coming years. I know that I will never forget the awesome and breathtaking scenery and the sense of accomplishment when we completed a very challenging trek. To do it with my special friends meant more than I can express.

And as for the skydiving all I can say is WOW!!!! I am so proud of both of us 50+ ladies doing something we dreamed of in our youth and so glad we did it together.

I think the reason I was not afraid was because I just knew it was the perfect time and therefore nothing could go wrong!

Chapter 34:
Turning 70

I felt so grateful turning 70 in 2014. I was as fit, healthy and probably as happy and contented as I'd ever been.

I decided to have a birthday get-together on a Sunday afternoon. We booked the function room at the Canadian Bay Hotel in Mt Eliza, where 130 fantastic, positive, enthusiastic people helped make this a day I'll never forget.

Five of my six children, Sheree, Kelly, Debbie, Adam and Rebekah, were with me along with our first granddaughter Ebony.

Of course, Sharyn organised everything to ensure that everyone had a great time. The energy in the room was amazing, with people from all parts of my complex life.

Adam wrote and read out a poem in his own personal and wonderful way.

Happy 70th Birthday

With the eye of the tiger, Ronnie's watching us all

Always there when we rise and when we fall

He turns 70 today and we're here to share

And show him we love him and how much we care

Full of advice for me for 33 years

He's been there for the joy and for the tears

"Take this pebble from my hand", he cried

Repeated over and over, I almost died

He's not a Kung Fu Master, and I didn't care

Giving him my best disinterested 'get over it' glare

Ronnie would not be put off, he had wisdom to impart

Full of shit mostly, but it's always from the heart

Don't trust people or horses with their eyes close together and more

Some of his lines were odd, and listening to him was often a bore

Except for advice from his Mother Marg

Whose legs were small, but her impact large

The best one of all came a little later on

"Happy Wife, Happy Life" was the mantra of Ron

Six children he's had and I'm the only son in the bunch

Also the least likely to throw a punch

Being a footy player or a boxer was never my thing

You'd find me six feet under before you'd get me in the ring

Megan can't be here today, but 5 out of 6 isn't bad

If someone told him this 15 years ago, he'd think they were mad

Debbie, Kelly and Sheree, I know how much your presence is felt

Your love and affection makes Ronnie's heart melt

Kelly says love, passion and integrity are the words that describe him best

Sounds like a tattoo you'd see on his chest

Sheree says he's an inspiration and she loves him dearly

The feeling is mutual, we can see that clearly

Joybell says he's determined, sensitive and kind

However, there are often times when she thinks he's lost his mind

As children go, I don't think he's done too bad

Although none of us know where the turtle is hidden, which still makes him sad

Joybell has always been the apple of his eye, his number one treasure

That is until Ebony came along which gave him so much pleasure

He showers his granddaughter with affection; she's the one he really loves

Ready to give her a boxing lesson and her own special gloves

When this child grows up and the boys (or girls) come knocking

The reaction of Ronnie and of Paul will potentially be shocking

Ronnie the boxer and Paul with his butchers' knife

Will make life hell for whoever wants to have her as their wife

Life Long Fitness and the Boxing Centre were a dream come true

Run on heart and soul, the business grew and grew

His clients have come and gone, some more special than others

Many of you have stayed and been like sisters and like brothers

He's met his match in Sharyn, it's a combination of love and fear

She scares us all sometimes, but he still holds her dear

He's always told me to be a verb

It's still the best advice I've ever heard

He lives this himself every single day

And when it comes to health and fitness he shows us the way

Today is your chance to celebrate and applaud all that is great

Ronnie is our father, our friend and always your best mate

Happy Birthday!

Chapter 35:
Out of our comfort zone

Sharyn and I have continued to travel and take ourselves out of our comfort zone.

We returned to New Zealand a couple of years later to explore the wonders of the North Island. We've visited America twice in the last two years as Adam, our son, has been living in Miami for three years and this has given us an insight into this very diverse lifestyle. We spent time apartment-living in Manhattan, exploring Washington DC, meeting Adam's colleagues in Washington, Miami and Baltimore as well as catching up with Australian friends now living in Los Angeles. We continue visiting Bali, monitoring the situation with Rya's eyes and ensuring ongoing care with the John Fawcett Foundation, as well as seeing our dear Balinese friends whom we now think of as our family.

In 2016 Sharyn, at the age of 59, in her words, "embarked on the beginning of a self-discovery journey". She flew on her own to Santiago, the capital of Chile in South America. She stayed overnight and under surreal circumstances, met Adam for the day when he was working in Brazil and decided to fly in to meet her in Chile. They spent a wonderful day together exploring museums, with lunch and dinner and a lovely catch-up. The following day she flew to Lima and then onto Cusco in Peru.

Within hours of arriving in Cusco she became unwell

with altitude sickness. Cusco is 3400 metres above sea level and the ninth highest city in the world. Sharyn was still unwell after three days, but decided to continue her plan to tackle the four-day trek to Machu Picchu along the famous Inca trail.

Prior to leaving Australia Sharyn had planned to meet up with her Australian niece (who for the last few years had been travelling frequently to Peru working with a volunteer organisation). On arrival, when she caught up with her married niece, she discovered that she was living a double life in Peru (with her husband back in Australia). She was partying hard and was too sick to join Sharyn on the trek.

The classic four-day Inca Trail is Peru's number one trek and one of the most well-known and popular treks in the world. Sharyn had booked with a tour company called Llama Path; her group consisted of 13 young people, mainly from the US, and a couple from Melbourne, as well as 28 porters and chefs and two trek leaders.

The four-day trek covers 45 kilometres and the starting altitude is 2720 metres above sea level, rising to the highest point on day two at Dead Woman's Pass, at 4217 metres. Sharyn struggled severely with altitude sickness, but the bond between the group, the magnificent scenery and the overwhelming feeling of ancient history contributed to one of the toughest yet best things she has ever done.

We have since met up with five members of the group in America and Australia and the feeling of connection was obvious. I am so convinced that putting ourselves way out of our comfort zone enables us to grow in all aspects of our lives.

Chapter 36:
The Boxer

In 2015, Jack Ahern, one of our boxing school boys and a Year 11 student at Mt Eliza Secondary College, asked if he could make a short film of our boxing centre for a school project.

Of course I agreed and he soon began his project.

Jack is a special young man and had already become a close friend to Sharyn and me over the last two or three years. He began a photography business named Driftwood Photography and his hobby of taking photos was turning into a small business alongside his studies.

Over the course of a few weeks Jack, in his quiet, unobtrusive way, began filming different aspects of our boxing centre.

One Saturday morning he came to our home and boxing centre accompanied by his dad, and recorded an interview. His dad was in charge of lighting and logistics.

They had previously filmed me shadow boxing, lifting weights and exercising in general. I had been quite comfortable with that part of the process.

In the interview Jack, as a young man ahead of his years with lots of feeling and sensibility, was able to ask me questions that forced me to delve into my past. Over the couple of hours that the interview took, I became emotional with guilt and embarrassment as I discussed my life's journey. I'm not proud of so many parts of my life. After the interview I left the entire process and content of the film totally to Jack.

A couple of weeks later I was able to see the preview of *The Boxer.*

It had a total WOW effect on me. He had tapped into my inner soul. I loved that he was able to capture my philosophy on peace and harmony and my relationships with discipline, self-respect, respect for others as well as boxing and martial arts.

He produced *The Boxer* on DVD and YouTube. To find *The Boxer* on YouTube, search for "The Boxer extended version" or "Mt Eliza Boxing Centre", then open *The Boxer (Extended Version).*

Jack designed the DVD cover using his photographs, and wrote the cover wording.

It's Not the Boxer That Makes the Man, but the Man That Makes the Boxer

The Boxer *is based on a true story which explores the life and personal philosophy of seventy-one-year-old Mt Eliza resident, personal trainer, and former professional boxer, Ron Smith. This film explores the ways in which the sport of boxing has impacted upon Ron's fascinating and inspiring life story and contributed to his personal philosophy.*

The documentary will not seek to glorify the inherent violence of boxing, but it will attempt to highlight the way that boxing has provided Ron with a sense of discipline – a capacity to control both his body and mind – which has helped him survive the various "rounds" of his life story. The film also explores

Ron's relationship with another boxer, Johnny Famechon (former Commonwealth Champion 1967 and former World Featherweight Boxing Champion 1969).

The documentary film presents a non-conventional boxing story that is more a story of harmony than it is destruction, as well as a film that will motivate the audience to question their own philosophy/purpose in their everyday lives.

Chapter 37:
Lifelong health and fitness

At 74 years of age, I'm fortunate to be in excellent health, working hard and living the dream. Sharyn and I have become a formidable team, working side by side in our businesses, The Centre for Lifelong Health and Fitness and the Mt Eliza Boxing Centre.

Our typical week begins early Monday morning with clientele ranging from seven years old to 83 – a vast range of people from all walks of life with a variety of goals, hopes, dreams, restrictions and excuses in a quest to be the best versions of themselves.

Tuesday mornings consist of putting John Famechon through his exercise routine at his home in South Frankston. It's a special time for us both.

Tuesday, Wednesday and Thursday afternoons between four and five o'clock, our schoolkids' boxing classes are a big hit for the 30-plus kids that attend, and a delight for me. I love watching these children develop from kids to young adults, maturing physically and mentally, developing respect for themselves and each other. To be in a position of influence to these young people is not something I take lightly, working closely with them, listening to their day-to-day issues ... challenges that are so different from the world I grew up in.

I have no doubt that the world is in a good place going forward, as the majority of these kids are far smarter than the generations before them. Issues such as the environment, equality, racism and bigotry (which is still ingrained in my generation) will be addressed by these current and future generations, including my very special grandchildren.

Our community radio work continues on the fourth Friday of every month, when Sharyn and I have a regular spot on a local program called *Mornings with Heather and Michelle*. We love being a part of the show with these two beautiful women. We talk about the wonderful lifestyle that's possible on the Mornington Peninsula, along with health, wellbeing and fitness amongst many other things, in a fun-filled program.

Working 12-hour days from Monday morning until lunchtime Friday we average 120 clients a week through our doors, including personal training, group and one-on-one boxing for adults and kids, nutrition, dietary advice, time management and life skills.

From midday Friday until Monday morning is catch-up time for Sharyn and me. My early morning year-round Saturday and Sunday morning swims in Port Phillip Bay are probably the best thing that I do for my body, mind and soul.

The simple things in life – being with our grandchildren, walking our dog to the beach and hanging out together after our busy week – are our solace. We love getting out in the garden and going for long bushwalks.

At the moment Sharyn's mum is living with us. She's only very recently been diagnosed with terminal cancer, but her positive attitude and sense of humour is unbelievable. She shows so much courage discussing her death, her funeral and her wishes, and we're determined to make this time for her as normal as possible. Lots of good food and the company of some of our special clients and friends are helping us make this time for her all about living and not dying.

Sharyn and I continue to work on our own personal self-development and growth, and putting ourselves out of our comfort zone.

Writing this book has done that for me. During the process, I've struggled with guilt and self-doubt, and all types of positive and negative emotions have surfaced.

I think it's really only the support of Sharyn, her mum, and my adult children and friends that have made the completion of this book about my journey to lifelong health and fitness a reality.

I feel blessed.

Where to from here?

I did it. Way out of my comfort zone, I wrote my memoir. That journey itself has made me reflect on what I've really learned over these 74 years.

Destiny is a function of chance and choice.

We create our own meaning of life.

We are the result of our life choices.

All actions have consequences.

Surround yourself with positive people.

Spend as much of your time with people who add value to your life and drag you up and not down.

Choose your company and friends wisely.

You can choose your friends but you can't choose your family.

I've been in a toxic relationship with some of my in-laws for more than 50 years; this caused enormous grief to both my parents and my partner, June.

My brother and sister, whom I love dearly, have been dominated by jealous, hostile partners for most of their lives and this has adversely affected our relationships. I'm searching within myself to understand their reasoning and find positives for this situation.

Yet apart from this negative part of my life, which has caused me so much grief, I have at last found peace within. I'm finally feeling blessed, happy and content in my life. Well then, where to from here?

To go into old age the best that I can be as a father, grandfather and husband.

To continue to grow as a person, and create my own meaning of life!

To continue learning and giving all that I am capable of.

In writing this book and analysing my sporting endeavours, I realise that without me ever thinking long term, I have been extremely fortunate that I've unknowingly spent a lifetime training for the main event ... my life!

I've thoroughly enjoyed the writing process and this has inspired me to consider my next venture: to write a book titled *Training for the MAIN EVENT ... Your life!*

I feel proud and blessed that, after leaving home and school at 13 years of age to go and ride a horse, in a roundabout way I found a life.

Special people in my life

Writing this book has made me think deeply about my adult children and the special people in my life. With their permission, I've decided to say a few words about each of them here, and some of them have contributed their own thoughts about me.

Adam

Adam was born an old soul. Smart from the start, and I ask myself constantly – how did he get here? These are some of the thoughts and feelings I remember about this very different kid.

In my mind, Adam was going to play football for Collingwood and become an Olympian. After having four beautiful and wonderful girls and being a pathetic father, this was my chance to live my life through Adam. How wrong I was. I was over the top with my endeavours to ensure my son was going to be a great athlete. The result was, it was not going to be, as Adam had two left feet, couldn't throw a ball or ride a bike and, most importantly, wasn't interested.

It was at a parent–teacher interview at Mt Eliza Secondary College that Sharyn and I sat with one of his teachers, who said, "This kid is something special. I'm not sure in what way but perhaps he will become an archaeologist or something out of the ordinary."

Adam continued with an unquenchable passion to learn and push boundaries in his quest for knowledge. Still at high school, he began volunteer work with Oz Child at 16 years of age.

Oz Child Services in Mornington has programs that range from foster care for children aged 0–18 who can no longer live with their natural parents; services for children with disabilities; health and welfare support such as counselling in schools and for families experiencing difficulties; respite for families whose children often have complex needs; and education, scholarships, mentorship and development programs for disengaged and underprivileged youth.

At about this time, Adam wrote to Dame Elizabeth Murdoch and applied for a grant to assist with a program he'd developed. The *Positive Role Models and Mentoring Program* was to be initiated at Oz Child, Mt Eliza Secondary College and Kunyung Primary School. He received a generous cheque for $5000 and the philanthropist in him was born.

Over the next couple of years Adam continued his amazing work with young people. Public speaking at corporate and not-for-profit organisations became his vehicle for spreading his message, and he was in high demand as a keynote speaker and radio and TV guest.

Some of the accolades he received during these years were the Young Citizen of the Year, Mornington Peninsula Shire; the City of Melbourne Award; and in 1999 and 2000, Adam was nominated and then shortlisted for the Young Australian of the Year.

It was such an honour for Sharyn and I to receive a personal invitation to attend the presentation dinner at the Hilton on the Park in Melbourne and to witness the extraordinary young talent in our country.

MEDIA RELEASE

YOUNG AUSTRALIAN TO SPEAK TO THE UNITED NATIONS

THE UNITED NATIONS YOUTH ASSOCIATION (UNYA) TODAY ANNOUNCED THE SELECTION OF ADAM SMITH FROM MELBOURNE AS THE AUSTRALIAN YOUTH REPRESENTATIVE TO THE 2003 UNITED NATIONS GENERAL ASSEMBLY.

Adam, aged 22, is a youth worker and youth development officer and also runs a business as an educational consultant.

He has worked with many youth and non-governmental organisations including the Coalition for the Homeless in New York City.

He is currently studying Education, Psychology and Business at Monash University in Clayton.

While in New York, Adam will be a fully accredited member of the Australian Delegation to the 58th United Nations General Assembly (UNGA).

His role will involve being an advocate for the views of young Australians. He will also be involved in the daily activities of the Australian mission and will deliver Australia's statement on Social Development and Youth to the UN.

Consultation with young Australians is an important part of the role. Adam is keen to engage the valuable views and perspectives of young people and to use the information he receives to shape his goals and priorities for his time in New York.

According to Adam, "In recent years it has become

increasingly evident that Australia's youth population has a remarkable opportunity to act as a catalyst for positive changes on a global scale. I am honoured to be able to represent the ideals of young people across Australia and am committed to doing this in a meaningful and proactive manner."

UNYA President Alyson Kelly highlighted the importance of youth participation in the UN, stating "Adam's work in New York will ensure that there is a voice for Australian youth in the UN. The youth representative position illustrates the government's recognition of the necessity of a youth presence in the global body.

Young people, not only can, but must play an important role in all levels of governance, including international organisations such as the UN."

The youth representative is chosen by young people to represent young people.

Adam was chosen from a large pool of impressive applicants and applications were open to all young Australians age 15–24.

Adam has continued to inspire, with his relentless work ethic in his endeavour to make the world a better place.

A recent job description and notification of a new role within Laureate Education sums up his latest exploits.

August 25, 2017

On January 3, 2018, Adam Smith will join Laureate Australia and New Zealand as General Manager, Education and Corporate Affairs.

For the past three years Adam has held the position of Executive Director, Global Public Affairs, based at Laureate's office in Miami, Florida. In this role, Adam led Laureate's global "Here for Good initiatives", helped establish Laureate as the world's largest B Corp and Public Benefit Corporation and led an international team responsible for media, external and executive communication, events, impact reporting, thought leadership, global non-profit partnerships, student experience and network awards and scholarships.

Prior to joining Laureate in 2014, Adam worked for 15 years in education and philanthropy in Australia, holding positions which included CEO of the Foundation for Young Australians, CEO of Education Foundation Australia, Chair of the Commonwealth Government's Family School Community Partnership Bureau, Board Member of the Australian Council of Educational Research and advisor to the Australian Curriculum, Assessment and Reporting Authority, Australian Institute of Teaching and School Leadership, Principals Australia Institute and the Bill and Melinda Gates Foundation.

In addition, Adam was a regular commentator on education-related issues on Channel 10's The Project *and on Radio 2GB, as well as a featured contributor in a range of newspapers and industry publications.*

Adam's work has always been guided by the belief that for individuals, communities and countries to thrive, nothing is more important than providing access to quality education. This is what led Adam to Laureate and what inspired him to assist in leveraging our global network to be a force for good in the world. As the co-founders of the B Corp movement often say, we need to move from aspiring to be the best in the world, to being the best for the world and this is true for our network, including here in Australia and New Zealand.

When asked what "Here for Good" means to him, Adam says "Here for Good is not a slogan or a catch cry. It's the expression of who we are and who we want to be. It's our commitment to measure and value our financial performance and our social impact. It's being creative in designing curriculum with both an academic and a social outcome. It's our desire to enjoy our work and feel complete alignment with our mission. It's what sets us apart."

As well as working with us on further extending our current "Here for Good" efforts, Adam will:

- *lead our education vertical, ensuring we continue to successfully grow this emerging area, becoming a trusted partner and a destination for students seeking a creative, competitive and inspiring advantage in the field of education*

- *lead Corporate Affairs, including internal and external communication, media, government relations and thought leadership*

- *continue to lead a number of global initiatives related to Here for Good, B Corp, and Laureate's partnership with the International Youth Foundation.*

"I couldn't be more pleased to be joining the Laureate Australia and New Zealand team. There's an exciting opportunity ahead of us to celebrate and share the

best of what you're currently doing with an entire network looking to collaborate with, learn from, and be inspired by you. I look forward to working with you on making this happen", said Adam.

Linda Brown
Laureate International Universities
CEO – Australia and New Zealand
President Torrens University

Adam continues to shine. Within our family he is still the same fun-loving son, grandson, brother and uncle to us all and he has never failed to remain in contact almost daily with his mother and grandmother.

On Mother's Day 2007 Sharyn asked Adam if he was gay. (She had previously asked him when he was 18.) His answer was yes.

I will never forget that day; I was out picking up his grandmother to bring her to our home for Mother's Day lunch. On arriving home Sharyn asked Adam to tell me the news. My first reaction was how to ensure his safety, as in my working life on construction sites I had often heard stupid men bragging that while drinking after work they would bash up "poofters".

I cuddled him and talked and cried. I had no idea about this way of life. I told him that I loved him and would support him in whatever way I could.

In the years since, Sharyn and I along with all our family have met so many of Adam's friends; beautiful, kind, caring and good people. In the early days when I heard stories of families, usually fathers, not accepting their gay sons these stories broke my heart. This amount of ignorance still hurts me today, especially with people of my generation, but thank goodness the younger generation are far smarter in accepting that we're all different in regard to nationalities, sexuality and so on.

Adam and his partner Omar were married in a private ceremony on the 24th of December 2017, both dressed in white, on a beach in Miami. We along with family and friends are so happy for them; the timing is perfect as they're moving to Australia for Adam to begin his new role as General Manager, Education and Corporate Affairs for Laureate Australia and New Zealand.

And the Australian government, after many years of debate and a somewhat divisive national postal survey, has recently passed a bill legalising same sex marriage.

Rebekah

Rebekah, our youngest daughter, lives close by in Mt Martha, a beautiful seaside village on Port Phillip Bay. She's married to Paul, a very hardworking butcher at his father's shop in Mt Eliza.

Rebekah and Paul have provided Sharyn and me with two wonderful granddaughters, Ebony Hope and Savannah Joy, the absolute love of our lives.

Words cannot describe the feeling and privilege that I have to be a positive influence and grandfather to these beautiful souls. I hope that the free spirits of these girls, who now dance and run with me with free abandon at two and five years of age, never leave them.

Rebekah is a special human being, a lovely, kind and caring person who over the past five years has devoted her life to her girls.

Surviving a very arduous start in life herself, and experiencing some difficult times growing up, Rebekah is a beautiful, gentle soul and wonderful, dedicated mother. Her grandfather Bernie would be as proud of her as I am.

Rebekah has had many struggles in life, primarily due to her prematurity. She had learning difficulties but managed to get through her years of education.

She changed schools in Year 10 and found a new sense of self-confidence after years of being bullied. After studying hard, she achieved her long-term dream of getting into university to study education. She attended Monash University in Frankston and achieved great results academically and during her placements.

She had dreams of teaching in underprivileged countries and making a difference to young people's lives. Unfortunately, she made the decision not to complete her last few months of study, and never completed her degree.

She went on to complete a Diploma in Professional Counselling and began her own business working with young children, which she ran for a brief time. She had a part-time job in a bakery to help support herself financially. She enjoyed dancing and had taken dancing lessons since she was three years old.

Rebekah discovered dancing and socialising at nightclubs with her friends. She was never a drinker, but enjoyed going out, having fun and meeting boys.

Rebekah and I were very close through her teenage years; I taught her boxing and self-defence; she was a master on the speed ball. We often ran together along the beach and bush tracks, and the foreshore between Seaford and Carrum.

Rebekah was a good athlete when we were alone, but when other people were around she struggled with self-confidence.

We also did some serious bush walking; Tasmania and Lorne are two places that come to mind, often walking across swollen creeks, out of our comfort zone, bonding and working as a team.

Now in her thirties, with maturity and being a mum and all that life has thrown at her, Rebekah has developed an air of calm self-confidence; she even recently got a tattoo on her arm.

With a spring in her step, it's a far cry from the young woman that struggled for years as a result of serious bullying through her teenage years.

I found a school piece written by Rebekah when she was just 16.

A special person

In doing my creative, reflective piece, I have chosen to think about a special person, what they mean to me, what qualities they possess and their flaws. This special person is my dad.

My dad's outlook on life is an inspiration to us all! Not many people would see him, or know him like I do and that is the amazing thing; we understand each other so well.

It hasn't been easy for him though; it took a long time of learning from many hard and challenging situations to reach the level he is currently at and without my mum this may never have happened. She helped him pull through and see through the hardships that he faced, she was there for him when he really needed someone to talk to. Without her he would not be who and where he is today.

My dad was once one of the best boxers in Australia and also very good at playing football when he was younger. He admits boxing is not the best sport to be involved in and the only reason he was involved with it in the first place was because it was something he was good at and so he followed this.

On the day I was born 16 years ago, all the nurses in the hospital were sure I was going to die. I was born 13 weeks premature. My dad however knew I was a fighter and would pull through; he had faith in me that I would survive. This belief never left him.

Since I was born Dad and I have never left each other's side. We've always been very close and have shared everything with one another.

As I have grown up, he has been there for me through times of unworthiness and of disappointment, through to times of happiness and times of success.

He has always been very committed to keeping fit and caring for his health. He used to be a dedicated long-distance runner, competing in a number of events and receiving a variety of different medals and trophies for his efforts. He now swims as he cannot run anymore due to problems concerning his knee. All this has impacted on me taking control of my health and fitness and using it in the best possible way I can. So now he can offer me advice on my health and on improving my running skills.

His only flaws would be that at times he tends to worry too much, which places a lot of unwanted pressure on himself. Still, nobody has characteristics within themselves that they cannot work on and improve. No one is perfect after all!

My dad has inspired me to become an individual and to be the best I can be, to have my own beliefs and to stick with them. All he ever wants is for me to be happy and he would give up his own life to make that possible.

He is the most positive, sensitive and most loving person in the entire world. He can see the bright side of any situation and can offer some special advice of what he already knows and has learnt to whoever is in need. He is always very comforting towards me and we share a lot in common. I admire him very much.

One thing's for sure, my dad has touched my life in a way that I could never describe and will be in my heart and in my dreams forever.

Sheree

The original free spirit, my eldest daughter Sheree doesn't fit into any box. She's a beautiful soul who lives life to the absolute fullest.

This dynamo lives in Byron Bay, a coastal town in northern NSW, with her partner Guy. In recent years she has been a marriage and funeral celebrant, as well as a long-time employee of Bunnings in various locations.

She recently put into words her memories of me.

My dad

One of my first memories as a child is going to visit my grandparents and my dad's father, sitting me on a stool in the kitchen near the fridge and him doing a magic trick, pulling a chicken's egg out of my ear. Of course this was the most amazing thing I had ever seen until that point in my life.

Another memory is Dad picking me up in the middle of the night and taking me across the street to my mum's parents' house and me climbing into the middle of the bed with my nana and pop.

I remember my dad putting raw eggs in a glass with other things, mixing it up and drinking it for breakfast and he would skip in the kitchen. The rope would go so fast and make a cracking noise and he would make it cross over in the front and I thought he was so clever.

I also remember sitting down with all the family at my great nana's house watching my dad on a little black and white TV screen in a boxing ring, boxing with another man.

Then we moved house from across the street from my nana to a new house at the bottom of a very big hill. I remember family picnics and holidays and many happy times. Then I remember one day my mum ironing my dad's shirts and putting his things in the car and us taking them to his work and her throwing them inside a little door of the workshop where he worked.

My dad was gone.

We went to live with my nana and pop and life was good and if ever the conversation turned to my dad I only ever heard good things. My nana would say, "Your dad was a good man but I think he got a few too many punches to the head." I can't remember specific things Mum said but it was always positive.

One of my favourite things to do was to crawl under

the house; I would spend hours down there looking through all the things stored in boxes. I will never forget the day that I found a box of my dad's stuff; it was full of trophies, most of them boxing trophies. I was so excited, carefully looking at everything and remembering my dad. I loved him and missed him.

I chose my favourite trophy, it wasn't like the others. Most of them where plastic gold men in boxing poses fixed to little wooden cubes. But this one was different. It was a silver cup with two little handles and it had the words Ron Smith: Best Boy of Tournament *engraved on it in fancy writing and I took it.*

I wasn't sure if I was allowed and I was too scared to ask in case they said no. This trophy was real, it made my dad real, and over the years I would hold the cup and wonder about my dad and where he was and what he was doing.

I moved out of home when I was 18 and by this time Mum had remarried; a few years later she moved away from the Diamond Valley area to Seaford with her husband Bruce and their children, my brother Jason and sister Michelle. When I was in my twenties they were in primary school and one day mum told me she had gone along on a school excursion with Michelle's class with a few other mum's. Apparently on the bus she started talking with another mum, telling her that she had three older daughters from her previous marriage ... We couldn't believe it but it turned out that she was talking to Sharyn, my dad's new wife. Also years later we found out that Mum lived across the road from a football oval that Dad often jogged around, the same oval where we took Jason and Michelle to play.

Over the years I often thought about looking for Dad but never did, then one day when I was 40 Kelly called and said she wanted to find Dad and did I want to find him too. I was keen but very surprised when she called me back a few days later to say that she had found him. Quite surprising considering his surname was Smith. Debbie came on board and we all arranged to meet. I flew down from NSW and Kelly, Debbie, baby Leah (Debbie's youngest daughter, who was 11 months old, which happened to be exactly the same age as Debbie was when we last saw Dad) and I all stood on Dad's front doorstep.

We were all very nervous standing at the door that was about to be opened by a man that was our father and his wife Sharyn, people that were strangers to us.

Although I was nervous I was also very happy to be there and in my handbag I had the trophy that I had held onto for over 30 years.

I remember lots of tears and hugs and smiles, awkwardness too, but the world was right again the moment Dad wrapped his arms around me.

It was wonderful to spend time with Dad getting to know him and Sharyn but the thing I found most amazing was to see the similarities that Dad and I shared.

I am at peace with my dad; I know he had a journey to travel and that he is the man he is today because of this journey and how he chose to face it. I accept it all and of course I am very, very happy to have Dad back in my life.

Don't get me wrong, I have often wondered what my life would have been like growing up with such a wonderful man as my dad around. But wisdom has taught me not to live in the past.

The love that Dad and I share is real and it's the greatest present I could ever have.

Kelly

My middle daughter Kelly is married to Steve. They've been together since high school and live in the Melbourne suburb of Greensborough. They have three adult children, Chris, Jamie and Chloe. Kelly and Steve have their own commercial and domestic cleaning business; they're hard workers, as running your own business is a tough gig. They part-own a boat with Bruce, Kelly's stepfather, and her stepbrother Jason. The boat is berthed at Yaringa Marina on Western Port Bay, so whenever possible and the weather is kind they are off fishing. They've recently bought a caravan and intend to do some serious travelling.

As with all of my children, Kelly has good values and is a credit to herself.

I asked Kelly if she could share her thoughts and emotions prior to making THAT phone call on the 8th of June 2004, around my sixtieth birthday. Her phone call changed a number of lives and relationships forever.

My dad/Ron asked me if I could write down some of my feelings about him when I was growing up. Also how I felt when I decided to look him up later in life.

Growing up, Dad wasn't a word used often in our house. We had a stepdad (and still do), however, we called him by his first name. You were hardly ever spoken about.

Nana would talk about you from time to time. (In a good way.) Mum rarely ever spoke of you. I will always remember her words – clear as day – Your dad wasn't around for long. However the time he was, he was a good dad to you three girls.

I must admit, because of her attitude, I never had bad feelings towards you.

The feelings that I did have were of wonder. I was never really sure if you existed or not. Sheree had a book when we were young, called My Father Can Fix Anything.

Every time I looked at it, I wondered if you really could.

I only have one real memory from when I was a child. A memory that I will treasure always. The only real memory that I referred to when thinking of you. Other than the ones that I made up from the few photographs that I had of us. It's a vision – like a little video that I have stored in my heart. We are away on a holiday somewhere. We are in an old car (probably not that old at the time). I was sitting on your lap in the driver's seat.

You said I could have a turn of the steering wheel. I started to move it from side to side quite quickly. You told me that I needed to move it more slowly, or the car would go all over the place. It was a big steering wheel and I'm sure that the car had a bench seat. I'm not sure if anyone else was in the car at the time! In my memory, that was irrelevant. As it was always "just you and me", our special time. I would have been about two or three at the time.

When I was older my auntie told me that I was always "Daddy's girl". I was apparently your shadow! She said wherever you went, I wanted to go.

Sheree was always "Nana's girl". Debbie was always "Mummy's girl". I was "Daddy's girl". However, Nana and Mummy were still around.

The next time you came up in my life I was 18 years old. Debbie had decided to write you a letter, with much encouragement from Nana. She told you in the letter that I had a baby boy. When I read your return letter to her, which was nice, I cried and cried. I think they were tears of sadness or more so the fact that I could see your handwriting for the first time. I actually believed that you existed. For some reason we didn't have contact again.

At the age of 37, I went on a camping holiday with my family. Our daughter was 12 at the time. Her schoolfriend came with us, so we had to take two cars. On the trip home, it was just the two girls and I.

The friend was telling us how her Mum and Dad had split up, and how hard she was finding it. I then proceeded to tell them the story of how my dad had left when I was young. My daughter had never really heard this, and was quite interested. As the next few weeks went by, I found myself thinking about you all of the time. Wondering what you were like and where you lived.

I became quite obsessed with thinking about you.

I asked Sheree and Debbie what they thought about me looking you up. I asked Mum if she minded. She said not at all and gave me an idea of where she thought you might live on the Peninsula somewhere.

I looked up Smith in the white pages – Ha ha! There were a few. However I went to the letter R and found a number. My thoughts were, could it be this easy? I had worked out that it would have been right around your 60th birthday. I decided to call you.

My heart was racing as the phone rang. Wondering if it could possibly be you.

The phone was answered – Hello, Ron Smith speaking – I opened my mouth and said hello – Did you have a daughter back in 1966 called Kelly? – You said, yes I did! We talked for a long time. I was so excited to tell you all about the grandchildren that you have.

That was truly a very special moment in my life. One that I will always cherish. I told the girls (Sheree and Debbie) about our conversation. We then promptly organised a date to come to your house and meet you and Sharyn.

The day the three of us travelled in the car together was truly special. So many different emotions going on.

We stood at your front door and as you opened it – I believe that you and Sharyn opened your hearts and your home to us. Such a beautiful day, full of tears and laughter.

I felt sadness for you, as I could see that you carried so much guilt from leaving us all those years ago. I could also see that you were nothing but proud of the women we had become.

The hardest person for me to tell (that I looked you up) was my stepdad. Probably even harder than it was calling you.

He accepted the knowledge with such good grace. Over the years we have got to know each other. There is so much more time that I want to spend with you.

We can never replace those childhood years, and all of the special moments in my life that you missed out on.

However, the past is the past. Let's leave it where it is. I am so grateful that you are now a part of my life.

You are truly a beautiful soul, I am so proud to know you and for you to call me your daughter.

Love you very much, Kelly. Xx

Debbie

Debbie is the youngest of my three kids with Zandra. She has struggled through her life until the last few years and battled serious health problems, two marriages and two divorces. Her first marriage produced three fantastic daughters, Hayley, Emma and Leah, and they have become a dynamic group of four amazing women.

Knowing what I know now, I believe my leaving Zandra and the three kids affected Debbie the most.

Debbie and the girls live in Langwarrin, about a 30-minute drive from us, and currently she works in the office of a family law practice in Mornington.

Her middle daughter, Emma, is a valuable member of our Thursday afternoon kids' boxing class.

Debbie and I have become very good mates after some ups and downs in our relationship. I always look forward to our catch-up lunches or dinners whenever we can manage the time.

She is a strong and independent woman whom I admire greatly and she is the most amazing mum to her three daughters. During some very tough health battles, she has shown resilience like I've never known and has managed to get on with life regardless.

The day we went to meet Ron was a very different experience for me compared to Sheree and Kelly; they were both very excited, I on the other hand was very angry and unsure about this meeting. The thought of a father leaving his kids and never looking back made me angry. I wanted to know why? How? How could he do this to me? But I thought if I was ever going to meet him I wanted to do it at the same time as the others. So I went. It was a bittersweet day for me. I had finally met the man who left me but I also found out where I came from! It was when Ron took us into his gym that it hit me; this person was so similar to me, my traits, similar thoughts, my genes! It hit me like a slap in the face; I was overwhelmed, I cried, this person, this is where I came from. The more I get to know him the more I realise how much we are on the same wavelength.

Writing the book with Sheree was such a healing process for me. It was all the things I learnt on this journey that led me to be able to let the anger go, to realise everybody is just trying to deal with things the best they can, that everybody is trying to deal with their own thoughts. I learnt that forgiveness can bring great rewards and by letting negative angry thoughts go literally changes your life. Now I am such a grateful, happy person with a friend that I call my dad.

Debbie and Sheree wrote a fantastic book in 2016 called *You Could Find Something Good in a Bag of Chook Shit – A Guide to Life.*

The story is about two sisters who grew up in the same family and circumstances, but dealt with things in very different ways. Through writing the book, Debbie and Sheree were able to transform their lives profoundly and I'm sure will assist others to do the same. I'm very proud of them both for laying their souls on the line.

Megan

Megan, June's daughter, lives in Newcastle with her husband Brendan, her son Nathan and daughter Jessica. A highly successful woman, she's close to completing a PhD titled "Postprandial impact of dietary protein in individuals with type 1 diabetes mellitus".

As well as managing a clinical research and care unit for type 1 diabetes at Newcastle Hospital, she has written and presented papers on type 1 diabetes overseas and within Australia. She has some extensive qualifications and titles: Bachelor of Nursing (Registered Nurse) (Honours); Paediatric Clinical Nurse Consultant; Specialist Paediatric Diabetes Educator; Credentialed Diabetes Educator; and current President of the Australian Diabetes Educators Association (NSW).

We don't see each other much, unfortunately, or have much contact. I can only hope our relationship becomes closer in time.

Elaine

Elaine Strong is Sharyn's mother and my 92-year-old mother-in-law. We've been part of each other's lives for 42 years. Elaine and Bernie, Sharyn's dad, were a great support to us when our kids were young and were always there when we needed help.

Sadly, Bernie passed away 28 years ago on Christmas Day, 1989. Up until his death, Adam and Rebekah had a wonderful relationship with their grandfather; sadly he did not see them grow into the amazing people that they are today. However, I'm sure that the short time he had with them his influence, courage and determination became a part of who they are to this day.

Over the years, Elaine came on our family holidays and was always good fun and a great help with Adam and Rebekah. She loves animals and occasionally, as a part of our travels, we would visit places to see animals and wildlife. She has an affinity with birds, especially cockatoos, and our kids still to this day laugh about Gran laughing and dancing with the cockies on our trips.

Sharyn and her mum have a very close, open and honest relationship. Over the many years, especially since her dad died, Sharyn has always been there for her mum, assisting with multiple medical and emotional issues. Elaine is a kind, loving and gentle soul and tough as an old boot, having had both knees replaced, shoulder surgery and countless other medical and surgical interventions.

When Elaine was 91, Sharyn and I bought and introduced her to an iPad and set her up with Facebook, Facetime, Google, internet banking and email. She's taken to it all like a duck to water. She had daily contact with

Adam on Messenger while he was living overseas, and uses Facetime regularly to enjoy 'face-to-face' contact.

Elaine is now 92 and has a terrific relationship with Rebekah; she adores her great-grandchildren, Ebony and Savannah. She has a special bond with Adam and Omar, who love her dearly.

Gran, as she is affectionately known in our family, still drives her car, goes to the gym/physio twice a week, walks daily, shops and cooks healthy and nourishing meals for herself. She's knowledgeable about local and world news, and loves watching rugby, AFL, tennis and horseracing on TV.

I enjoy our chats together as she and I are only 18 years apart and we can relate to many events and people from a bygone era.

The health challenges Elaine currently faces are enormous, but her spirit, willpower and humour remain an inspiration.

Zandra and Bruce

Zandra and Bruce, Sheree, Kelly and Debbie's mother and stepfather, have been very understanding and kind following Kelly's phone call on my sixtieth birthday. I'm sure the relationship I now have with my three girls would have been much more difficult if Zandra and Bruce weren't as accommodating. Thank you both sincerely.

Josh

I first met Josh in May 2011, when he was 10 years old and his mum Sharon brought him along to a kids' boxing class. He was just one of many young boys learning to box and trying to get fit, but from day one I felt that this kid was something special.

At about the same time, his dad Mark and uncle Peter were regulars at the adult group boxing sessions. Sharon, his mum, was a natural athlete like her brother Peter and was a regular with our women's boxing group.

A couple of years after he started coming to our group sessions, I was having a tough time keeping myself together, as some of the boys were being even naughtier than usual. Although I didn't show the emotion I was feeling, in my mind I was thinking of giving up the kids' groups as I was finding them a huge challenge. At the end of the session the boys all left, unaware that I was so upset. It wasn't until I began the next session of men's and women's group boxing that I realised Josh was still in the gym, cleaning up the mess, and stacking the equipment the kids had left all over the floor and outside the gym.

Josh, though young in years, had picked up that I was upset. I thanked him and that night rang his mum and told her the story of how her beautiful and empathetic son had helped an old bloke going through a tough time. I asked her if I could employ Josh to help with the kids' sessions three afternoons a week.

That was four years ago. Josh now helps me run five sessions a week – three kids' groups and two adult classes. He's developed into a wonderful young man and a very popular part of our team. Sharyn and I think of him as part of the family.

He's also developed exquisite boxing skills; he and I have put together several videos that have included correct boxing technique instruction on our Mt Eliza Boxing Centre Facebook page and YouTube channel.

Watching him teach very young girls and boys, along with teenagers who quite often struggle with low self-confidence and lack of athletic coordination and ability, makes my heart melt; he has such a beautiful way about him. We often joke that his hair will turn grey soon like mine with the stress of managing some of the kids.

Josh has an old head on his young shoulders and has gone through his fair share of trauma, with the breakdown of family relationships and even a broken heart that most teenagers experience at some point in their complex lives.

I feel very fortunate to have been a part of Josh's journey from a 10-year-old boy to a very popular and respected young man in our community.

Sharyn

Sharyn has been my wife, partner, soulmate and best friend for 42 years. After a rocky start and the trials and tribulations of bringing up our children, the deaths of Bernie, Sharyn's dad, and my mum Marg, she has supported me in all my ups and downs, in my personal battles with alcohol, sporting endeavours and different career paths. I'm sure that I would never have made my fortieth birthday without her unwavering support, intelligence and unquestionable honesty with herself and those around her.

We've been exceptionally lucky, as we're quite different from each other, brought up in very different worlds and circumstances. Sharyn's parents didn't drink and she was the youngest of three much older siblings from whom, unfortunately, she has been estranged for many years.

Although vastly different in many ways, Sharyn and I

have, over time and with the hindsight of maturity, shared similar ideals and values about spirituality, equality for humankind, the environment, taking responsibility for our own health and wellbeing, and that all actions have consequences.

We're still learning and striving to be the best versions of ourselves, hoping to pass on the importance of being honest with ourselves and others, valuing compassion, and treating all people as we'd like to be treated.

Ron and Bernie

The final special people to mention on my journey are long since gone. However, as destiny would have it and without ever knowing each other, my father Ron Smith and Sharyn's father Bernie Strong shared a common bond that no one would know until decades later. It wasn't until quite recently that I obtained their personal Defence Service Records from the National Archives of Australia.

My father, Ron Smith, enlisted with the Australian Military Forces at the Melbourne Town Hall on 22 June 1940. Sharyn's father, Bernie Strong, enlisted with the Australian Military Forces at the Caulfield Town Hall on 25 June 1940.

Three days apart, embarking on a journey that would change their lives forever.

Both were sent to the Middle East. My dad became Private VX34907, 2nd/24th Battalion. Sharyn's dad became Private VX40732, 26th Anti-Tank Company, unit of 26th Infantry Brigade, 2nd/23rd, 2nd/24th, 2nd/48th Infantry of the 9th Australian Division. They were both in the 2nd/24th Battalion at some stage.

Sharyn's dad was shot in the left and right thighs and suffered a fractured left femur on 17 May 1941. My dad was wounded with a bullet through his left leg on 26 October 1942. Though more than a year separated their injuries, both ended up at the Heidelberg Repatriation Hospital in Melbourne.

Neither of our dads ever discussed the war, nor any details of their time in the military.

The Centre for
Lifelong Health and Fitness

Mission Statement

To provide an enjoyable and positive
experience to every person, every time.

To assist clients to manage their lives
in the best way possible for them,
to be the best version of themselves
regardless of genetics, age or past lifestyle.

To always encourage, assist and develop.

- the centre for -
Lifelong Health & Fitness

www.lifelonghealthandfitness.com.au

Printed in Great Britain
by Amazon